Cuisinart
Ice Cream
Recipe Book

By Nicholas J Lima

Copyright © by Nicholas J Lima

All rights reserved. No part of this book may be reproduced, distributed, or transmitted in any form or by any means, including photocopying, recording, or other electronic or mechanical methods, without the prior written permission of the publisher, except in the case of brief quotations embodied in critical reviews and certain other noncommercial uses permitted by copyright law.

Chapter

Quick & Easy

Creamy Frozen Yogurts

Gourmet Gelatos

Vegan Ice cream

Fruity Favorites

Kid-Friendly Flavors

Dreamy Chocolate Delights

Adult Friendly

Refreshing Sorbets & Sherbets

Holiday Flavors

Quick & Easy

Creamy Frozen Yogurts

Gourmet Gelatos

Vegan Ice cream

Fruity Favorites

Kid-Friendly Flavors

Dreamy Chocolate Delights

Adult Friendly

Refreshing Sorbets & Sherbets

Holiday Flavors

TABLE OF CONTENT

Introduction: 19
How to Use Your Cuisinart Ice Cream Maker? 20
Cuisinart Ice Cream Maker Maintenance 22

QUICK & EASY 25

1. Creamsicle Ice Cream 25
2. Pumpkin Marshmallow Ice Cream 25
3. Fresh Mint Ice Cream 26
4. Lavender Ice Cream 26
5. Salted Caramel Ice Cream 27
6. Caramel Apple Ice Cream 28
7. Butterscotch Ice Cream 29
8. French Vanilla Ice Cream 29
9. Vanilla Bean Honey Ice Cream 30
10. Cheesecake Ice Cream 30

CREAMY FROZEN YOGURTS 31

11. Vanilla Bean Frozen Yogurt 31
12. Chocolate Greek Yogurt Ice Cream 31
13. Vanilla Frozen Yogurt with Chocolate Swirl 32
14. Healthy Raspberry Frozen Yogurt 33
15. Lemon Frozen Yogurt 33
16. Lavender Frozen Yogurt 34
17. Berry Coconut Frozen Yogurt 34
18. Peach and Pistachio Frozen Yogurt 35
19. Mint Chip Frozen Yogurt 35
20. Mango Lassi Frozen Yogurt 36
21. Honey Almond Frozen Yogurt 36

GOURMET GELATOS 37

22. Authentic Italian Gelato 37
23. Dark Chocolate and Nutella Gelato 38
24. Pistachio Stracciatella Gelato 39
25. Sicilian-Style Gelato 40
26. Rhubarb gelato 41
27. Vegan Raspberry Rose Gelato 42
28. Vanilla Milk Gelato 42
29. Eggnog Gelato 43
30. Mango Gelato 44
31. Coffee Gelato 45

VEGAN ICE CREAM 46

32. Vegan Coconut Raspberry Ice Cream 46
33. Vanilla Bean Coconut Ice Cream 46
34. Vegan Mint Chocolate Chip Ice Cream 47
35. Vegan Chocolate Cherry Ice Cream 48
36. Vegan Pistachio Ice Cream 49
37. Vegan Chai Ice Cream 50
38. Avocado Ice Cream 51
39. Vegan Coffee Ice Cream 51
40. Vegan Butter Pecan Ice Cream 52
41. Vegan Cinnamon Ice Cream 53

FRUITY FAVORITES 54

    42. Peach Ice Cream 54
    43. Strawberry Ice Cream 54
    44. Passion Fruit Ice Cream 55
    45. Lemon Blueberry Cheesecake Ice Cream 56
    46. Healthy Blood Orange Ice Cream 57
    47. Blackberry Ice Cream 57
    48. Banana Berry Ice Cream 58
    49. Watermelon Mint Ice Cream 58
    50. Fresh Blueberry Ice Cream 59
    51. Coconut-Pineapple Ice Cream 59

KID-FRIENDLY FLAVORS 60

    52. Cinnamon Toast Crunch Ice Cream 60
    53. Circus Animal Cookie Ice Cream 61
    54. Cotton Candy Ice Cream 61
    55. Rainbow Sherbert 62
    56. Vanilla Ice Cream 63
    57. Fruity Pebbles Ice Cream 63
    58. Birthday Cake Ice Cream 64
    59. Candy Cane Ice Cream 64
    60. Caramel Corn Ice Cream 65
    61. Bubble Gum Ice Cream 66

DREAMY CHOCOLATE DELIGHTS 67

    62. Healthy Chocolate Ice Cream 67
    63. Dark Chocolate Fudge Ice Cream 67
    64. Mint Chocolate Chip Ice Cream 68
    65. Chocolate Hazelnut Ice Cream 69
    66. Cherry Chocolate Chunk Ice Cream 70
    67. Chocolate Orange Ice Cream 71
    68. Strawberry Chocolate Swirl Ice Cream 71
    69. Dark Chocolate Ice Cream 72
    70. Chocolate Fudge Brownie Ice Cream 73
    71. Cherry Chocolate Chip Ice Cream 74

ADULT FRIENDLY 75

    72. Baileys Ice Cream 75
    73. Tequila Lime Ice Cream 76
    74. Amaretto Ice Cream 76
    75. Red Wine Ice Cream 77
    76. White Russian Ice Cream 77
    77. Triple Gingerbread Ice Cream 78
    78. Rum Raisin Ice Cream 79
    79. Coffee Heath Bar Ice Cream 80
    80. Vanilla Bourbon Ice Cream 81
    81. Whiskey Ice Cream 82
    82. Lemon Basil Sorbet 83
    83. Tangerine Gelato 83
    84. Watermelon Mint Sorbet 84
    85. Orange Thyme Sorbet 84
    86. Mixed Berry Sorbet 85
    87. Pineapple Coconut Sorbet 85
    88. Mango Sorbet 86

- 89. Grapefruit & Honey Sorbet 86
- 90. Raspberry Sherbet 87
- 91. Coconut lime sorbet 87

HOLIDAY FLAVORS 88

- 92. Hot Chocolate Ice Cream with Marshmallows 88
- 93. Gingerbread Ice Cream 89
- 94. Ginger Maple Miso Ice Cream 89
- 95. Pumpkin Pie Ice Cream 90
- 96. Chai Latte Ice Cream 90
- 97. Rhubarb Ice Cream 91
- 98. Pistachio Ice Cream 92
- 99. Apple Cider Sorbet 92
- 100. Cardamom Plum Sorbet 93
- 101. Lemon Custard Ice Cream 94

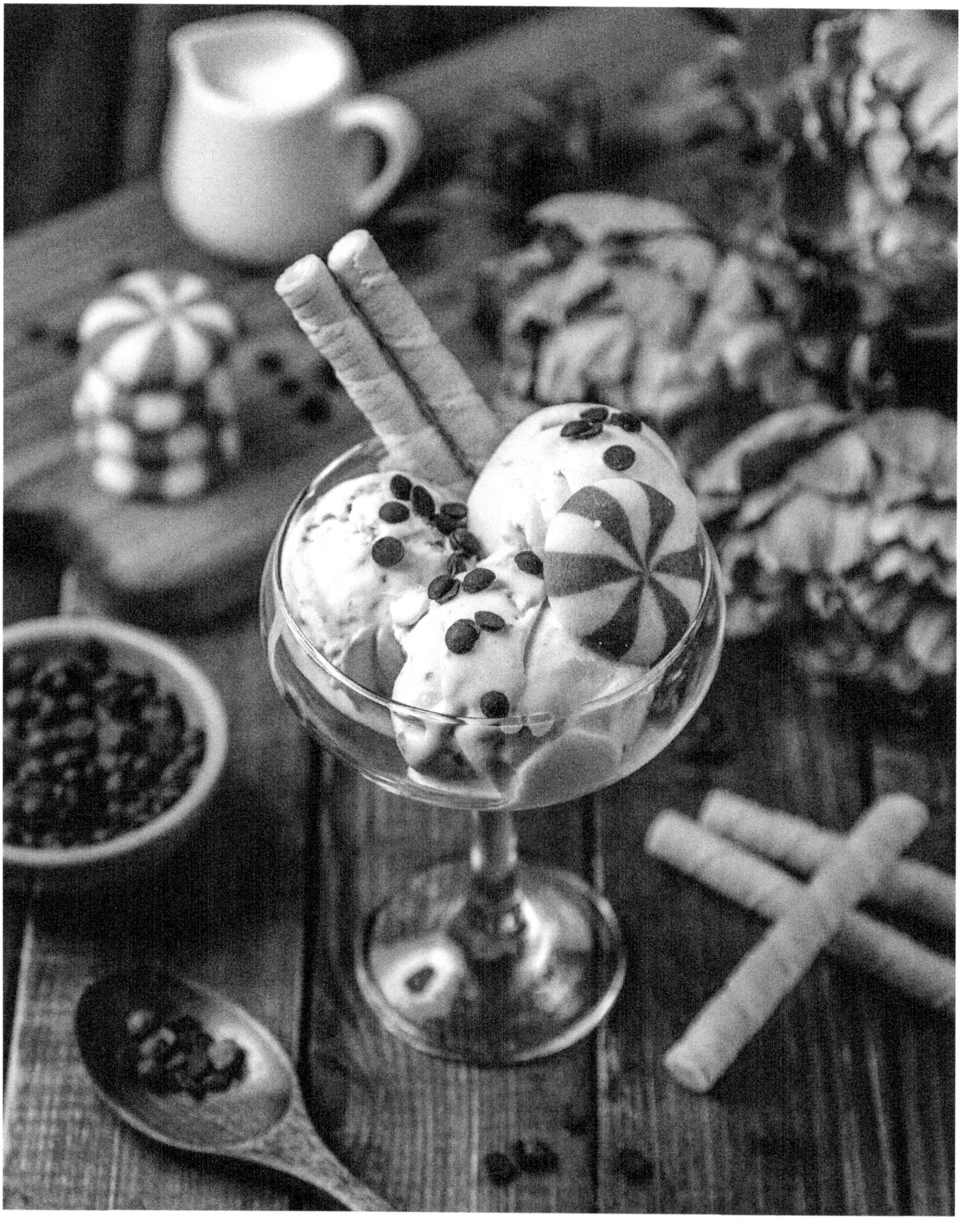

Introduction:

Welcome to the "Cuisinart Ice Cream Recipe Book," your ultimate guide to creating delectable frozen desserts that will turn your kitchen into a paradise of indulgence. Whether you're a seasoned ice cream enthusiast or just starting your journey into the world of homemade frozen treats, this book is designed to inspire and delight you, offering various recipes that cater to every taste and occasion.

In today's fast-paced world, there's something extraordinary about slowing down to craft your own ice cream, gelato, or sorbet from scratch. With the help of your trusty Cuisinart ice cream maker, you'll discover just how easy and satisfying it is to whip up creamy, dreamy desserts right in your own home. This book is packed with 100 meticulously tested recipes, each promising a perfect balance of flavour, texture, and creativity.

We've divided the recipes into thoughtfully curated categories to make finding exactly what you're craving easy. From Quick & Easy recipes that allow you to enjoy a frozen treat in no time to Creamy Frozen Yogurts that are light and luscious, this book has something for everyone. Dive into Gourmet Gelatos for a rich and velvety experience, or explore the Vegan Ice Cream section for dairy-free delights that don't compromise taste.

Our Fruity Favorites offer refreshing natural sweetness for fruit lovers, while the Kid-Friendly Flavors will surely be a hit with the little ones. Chocolate lovers will revel in the Dreamy Chocolate Delights, and adults can indulge in sophisticated flavours from our adult-friendly collection. Cool off with our Refreshing Sorbets & Sherbets on hot summer days, or bring festive cheer to your table with the Holiday Flavors.

"Ice Cream Heaven" is more than just a recipe book; it is an invitation to explore the art of dessert making, experiment with new flavours, and create sweet memories with loved ones. So grab your Cuisinart, pick a recipe, and craft heavenly desserts!

How to Use Your Cuisinart Ice Cream Maker?

Using your Cuisinart Ice Cream Maker is a simple and rewarding process that allows you to easily create delicious homemade ice cream, sorbets, gelatos, and frozen yoghurts. Follow these steps to get started:

1. Prepare the Freezer Bowl

Freeze the Bowl: The Cuisinart Ice Cream Maker uses a unique double-insulated freezer bowl to churn and freeze your mixture. To confirm that your ice cream turns out perfectly, place the freezer bowl in your freezer at least 12 to 24 hours before making ice cream.

The bowl should be completely frozen, which you can check by shaking. If you don't hear any liquid moving inside, it's ready.

2. Prepare Your Ingredients

Choose a Recipe: Select the recipe you'd like to make. Ensure all ingredients are chilled before starting, which helps the mixture freeze more quickly during churning.

Mix Ingredients: To mix the ingredients, follow the directions in the recipe. To get the best results, mix them well and put the mixture in the fridge for at least an hour before you churn it.

3. Set Up the Ice Cream Maker

Assemble the Machine: Place the frozen bowl on the base of the ice cream maker. Insert the paddle (dasher) into the centre of the bowl, then attach the clear plastic lid.

Turn on the Machine: Start the ice cream maker by pressing the "On" switch. The paddle will begin to rotate.

4. Add the Ice Cream Mixture

Pour in the Mixture: Slowly pour your chilled mixture into the freezer bowl through the lid's opening while the machine runs. This makes sure that the mixture is frozen and churned evenly.

5. Churn and Freeze

Churn the Ice Cream: Allow the machine to churn the mixture for 15-20 minutes. The time may vary depending on your recipe and the consistency you desire. The mixture will thicken and take on a soft-serve consistency as it churns.

Keep an eye on the process: Watch the ice cream as it's being stirred. Once it reaches the consistency you want, you can serve it right away as soft-serve or put it in a container that won't let air in to make it firmer.

6. Freeze for Firmer Ice Cream

Optional Freezing: For a firmer texture, transfer the ice cream to a freezer-safe container and freeze it for 2-4 hours or until it hardens to your liking.

7. Enjoy Your Homemade Ice Cream

Serve and Store: Scoop your homemade ice cream into bowls or cones and enjoy! If you have leftovers, store them in an airtight container in the freezer. Homemade ice cream is good to consume within a week for optimal flavour and texture.

Tips for Success

Pre-Chill Ingredients: Chilling your ingredients before adding them to the ice cream maker can help the mixture freeze faster and more evenly.

Avoid Overfilling: Don't overfill the freezer bowl. Leave some space for the mixture to expand as it freezes.

Keep the Bowl Frozen: After using, clean the bowl and return it to the freezer so it's always ready for your next batch.

You can use your Cuisinart Ice Cream Maker to make tasty frozen treats at home with these easy steps. The process and the sweet results are yours to enjoy!

Cuisinart Ice Cream Maker Maintenance

Proper maintenance of your Cuisinart Ice Cream Maker ensures its longevity and helps you consistently produce delicious frozen desserts. Here are the key steps to maintaining your machine:

1. Cleaning After Each Use

Unplug the Machine: Ensure the machine is unplugged before cleaning to avoid accidents.

Disassemble the Parts: Remove the freezer bowl, paddle (dasher), and lid from the base. These parts should be cleaned separately.

Wash the Freezer Bowl: Hand wash the freezer bowl with warm, soapy water. Avoid using abrasive cleaners & scouring pads that can damage the bowl's surface. Rinse thoroughly and dry completely before storing. Please do not submerge the freezer bowl in water or put it in the dishwasher, as this can damage the insulation and prevent proper freezing.

Clean the Paddle and Lid: Warm, soapy water can be used to clean the paddle and lid. Most of the time, they can go in the dishwasher, but check the manual for your model to be sure. Make sure they are thoroughly rinsed and dry before putting them away if you wash them by hand.

Wipe Down the Base: The motor base should never be immersed in water. Instead, wipe it down with a damp cloth and dry it immediately. Ensure no moisture enters the motor housing.

2. Storing the Freezer Bowl

Dry Thoroughly: After cleaning, ensure the freezer bowl is completely dry before returning it to the freezer. Any residual moisture can freeze and affect the bowl's performance.

Store in the Freezer: For optimal results, always store the freezer bowl in your freezer. This way, it's always ready for your next batch of ice cream. Keep it in a plastic bag to prevent ice crystals or frost from forming on the surface.

3. Regular Maintenance Checks

Inspect the Paddle and Lid: Regularly check the paddle and lid for any signs of wear or damage. If you notice cracks or wear, consider replacing these parts to maintain the machine's efficiency.

Check the Power Cord: Periodically inspect the power cord for any signs of damage. If you notice any fraying or wear, contact Cuisinart for a replacement or service.

4. Long-Term Care

Avoid Overuse: Give the machine adequate time to cool down between batches, especially if you're making multiple batches of ice cream. Overuse can cause the motor to overheat.

Service When Needed: If the machine starts to act up or the motor makes too much noise, look in the user manual for tips on fixing the problem. If the problem continues, call Cuisinart's customer service to have it fixed or maintained by a professional.

5. Off-Season Storage

Store in a Dry Place: If you don't use the ice cream maker for an extended period, store all parts in a cool, dry place. Ensure the freezer bowl is dry before storing it outside to prevent mould or odours.

Following these maintenance tips ensures your Cuisinart Ice Cream Maker remains in excellent working condition, ready to churn out delicious frozen treats whenever the craving strikes!

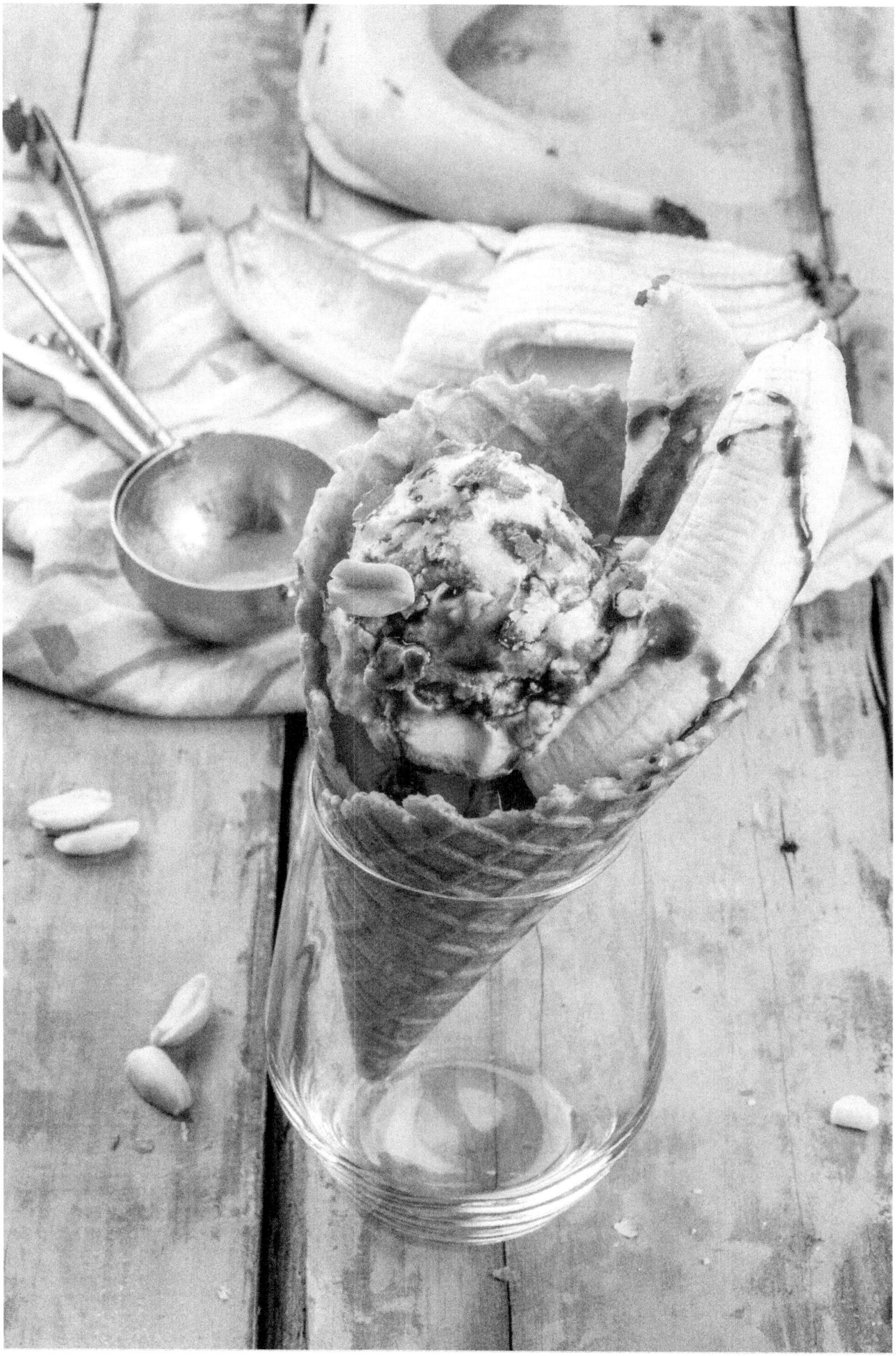

QUICK & EASY

1. CREAMSICLE ICE CREAM

Prep Time: 10 Minutes | Cook Time: 30 Minutes

Total Time: 40 Minutes | Serving: 6

Ingredients

- pinch of salt
- 1 1/2 cups of sugar
- 1 cup of whole milk
- 1 cup of half and half
- 1 tsp orange extract
- 1 1/2 cup of whipping cream
- 1 cup of orange juice fresh
- 1 Tbsp vanilla extract

Instructions

1. Mix everything and stir until the sugar is gone.
2. Put into an ice cream maker & follow the manufacturer's instructions for how to make ice cream.

2. PUMPKIN MARSHMALLOW ICE CREAM

Prep Time: 30 Minutes | Cook Time: 00 Minutes

Total Time: 30 Minutes | Serving: 6

Ingredients

- ¾ cup of granulated sugar
- 2 ½ cups of heavy cream
- 1 cup of marshmallow fluff
- 1 ½ cups of milk
- ¾ cup of pumpkin puree
- 1 tsp ground cinnamon
- 2 tsp vanilla extract

Instructions

1. Mix all the ingredients in a saucepan over medium-low heat with a whisk. Heat the mixture and stir it occasionally until the sugar is dissolved and the whole thing is warm.
2. Take it off the heat and let it cool down all the way.
3. Put it in the ice cream maker and churn it according to the directions on the box. Add 1/2 cup of marshmallow fluff and mix it in one last time right before the ice cream is done.
4. Put into a bowl that can go in the freezer, and then fold in the rest of the marshmallow fluff. Put the lid on top and freeze for about two hours or until the food is firm.
5. Take a scoop and enjoy!

3. FRESH MINT ICE CREAM

Prep Time: 20 Minutes | Cook Time: 20 Minutes | Total Time: 40 Minutes | Serving: 8

Ingredients
- 2 packed cups of mint leaves
- Pinch of salt
- 3/4 cup of sugar
- 1 cup of whole milk
- 2 cups of heavy cream
- 4 egg yolks

Instructions
1. Mix the milk, salt, sugar, and 1 cup of heavy cream in a pot. Heat over medium-low heat and stir the mixture often until it's all mixed. Toss the mint leaves into the hot milk and add them all at once. Turn off the heat, cover the pot, and wait for the milk to cool down. Once it reaches room temperature, cool it in the fridge overnight.
2. Put the mixture through a fine-meshed sieve the next day. It's fine if a few tiny mint leaf bits are in there. Bring the mixture back to a medium-low temperature. In a bowl, beat the egg yolks. Put the fine-mesh strainer over the other cup of heavy cream in a different bowl. When the mint-cream mix is about 150°F hot, it's time to temper the eggs. Whisk the eggs with one hand as you slowly pour in a ladle of hot cream. This needs to be done three times, mixing and pouring each time. After that, add the egg-cream mixture to the pot and mix it well.
3. While cooking slowly, stir until it gets thick enough to stick to a spoon. This should take about 160°F. Strain it and pour it into the bowl with the other cup of heavy cream. This will cool it down quickly. Put everything in the fridge and churn it as your ice cream maker says.

4. LAVENDER ICE CREAM

Prep Time: 30 Minutes | Cook Time: 20 Minutes | Total Time: 50 Minutes | Serving: 10

Ingredients
- pinch of salt
- ½ cup of granulated sugar
- 2 tbsp honey
- 2 tsp vanilla extract
- 2 cups of heavy cream
- 1 cup of whole milk
- ⅓ cup of lavender syrup

Instructions
1. In a large mixing bowl, whisk together all of the ingredients. Chill overnight or at least two hours prior to mixing in the ice cream maker.
2. Transfer the chilled ice cream mixture to your ice cream maker. Churn according to the manufacturer's instructions provided. Usually 15-20 minutes churning until your desired consistency. If you want the ice cream to be thicker, put it in a container that can go in the freezer and chill it for another one to two hours.

5. SALTED CARAMEL ICE CREAM

Prep Time: 10 Minutes | Cook Time: 30 Minutes

Total Time: 40 Minutes | Serving: 8

Ingredients

Vanilla Ice Cream:

- 1 1/2 cups of sugar
- 1/4 tsp salt
- 2 cups of whipping cream
- 1 1/2 cups of half and half
- 1 1/2 cups of whole milk
- 1 1/2 Tbsp vanilla

Salted Caramel Sauce:

- 3 Tbsp butter
- 1 cup of brown sugar
- 1/3 cup of whipping cream
- 1/4 cups of light corn syrup
- 1/2-1 tsp coarse French salt
- 1 tsp vanilla

Instructions

1. Whisk all of the ingredients together in a large bowl. Put it in the fridge overnight or at least two hours before you use an ice cream maker to mix it.
2. Put the chilled ice cream mix into the machine that makes ice cream. Follow the manufacturer's instructions for churning. Usually, you have 15 to 20 minutes of churning until the consistency you want is reached. If you want the ice cream thicker, put it in a container in the freezer and chill it for one to two hours.

6. CARAMEL APPLE ICE CREAM

Prep Time: 30 Minutes | Cook Time: 15 Minutes

Total Time: 45 Minutes | Serving: 12

Ingredients

- ⅓ cup of Smuckers Caramel Flavored Topping
- 2 tbsp butter
- 1 cup of apple cider
- 2 cups of peeled cooking apples
- 1 can of Sweetened Condensed Milk
- 1 ½ cups of half-and-half cream
- ¾ tsp apple pie spice

Instructions

1. Melt the butter in a large skillet over medium-low heat and add the apple. Cook the apple for about 10 minutes, stirring now and then, until it is soft. Add apple cider and apple pie spice, mix well, then cover and let it cook for 5 minutes.
2. If you put sweetened condensed milk and cream in a medium bowl, mix them using a whisk. Add the apple mix and stir. Add ice cubes and very cold water to a large bowl until it's about half full. Place the ice cream mix bowl in the middle of the large bowl. It will take about 5 to 10 minutes of stirring until it is very cold.
3. Follow the steps that came with your ice cream maker to freeze it. Put it in a square pan that is 8 or 9 inches square. Put the lid on top and freeze for about three hours or until the food is firm. Put a lot of ice cream in the pan after scooping it out. Spread the caramel topping over the whole top, letting it seep into the ice cream. Put the ice cream back in the pan. Put the lid on it and freeze it until you're ready to serve.

7. BUTTERSCOTCH ICE CREAM

Prep Time: 20 Minutes | Cook Time: 25 Minutes

Total Time: 45 Minutes | Serving: 10

Ingredients
- 1 cup of brown sugar
- 2 tsp vanilla extract
- 2 cups of heavy whipping cream
- 1 cup of milk
- 2 tbsp butter

Instructions
1. Mix sugar, vanilla, and butter in a large saucepan.
2. Put the mixture on medium heat and heat it until it starts to bubble.
3. Put half a cup of milk and stir it in again and again until it's smooth.
4. Take it off the heat.
5. Mix well with the heavy whipping cream and the rest of the milk.
6. Put it in the fridge for at least three hours.
7. Put the butterscotch mixture that has been chilled into your ice cream maker.
8. Mix in an ice cream maker for about 25-30 minutes or as directed by the maker.
9. Enjoy! Serve with toppings if you like!

8. FRENCH VANILLA ICE CREAM

Prep Time: 25 Minutes | Cook Time: 00 Minutes

Total Time: 25 Minutes | Serving: 8

Ingredients
- 2 cups of heavy whipping cream
- 1 cup of milk
- 2 large eggs
- 3/4 cup of sugar
- 2 tsp vanilla extract

Instructions
1. Whisk the eggs in a bowl for one to two minutes until they are light and fluffy.
2. Slowly add the sugar while whisking. Keep whisking for another minute or so until the sugar is completely mixed in. It is essential to add the cream, milk, and vanilla and mix them with a whisk.
3. Put the mixture in an ice cream maker and freeze it according to the machine's directions.
4. Add 1 cup of coarsely chopped Reese's Peanut Butter Cups for a different flavour, and let the ice cream keep processing after it gets stiff.

9. VANILLA BEAN HONEY ICE CREAM

Prep Time: 10 Minutes | Cook Time: 20 Minutes

Total Time: 30 Minutes | Serving: 10

Ingredients
- 2 vanilla beans
- 4 cups of half & half
- 2/3 cup of honey

Instructions
1. In a saucepan, mix the half-and-half and honey. Cut the two vanilla bean pods in half with a sharp knife, then scrape all the seeds. Put it in the pot.
2. Over medium heat, stir the mixture until it starts to bubble. Take it off the heat and wait an hour for it to cool. Mix it up every once in a while.
3. Put the mixture in a bowl with a lid and put it in the fridge overnight.
4. Pour the mix through a sieve into your ice cream maker the next day. Follow the directions that come with it.
5. Put the ice cream in a container that won't let air in and freeze it for an hour.
6. Serve and enjoy!

10. CHEESECAKE ICE CREAM

Prep Time: 10 Minutes | Cook Time: 00 Minutes

Total Time: 10 Minutes | Serving: 6

Ingredients
- 2/3 cup of sugar
- 1 lemon scrubbed clean
- 1/2 cup of half and half
- 1/8 tsp kosher salt
- 1 cup of sour cream
- 8 ounces cream cheese

Instructions
1. Put the cream cheese in the blender after cutting it up. After putting the lemon zest right into the blender, set the lemon aside to use another time. Mix in the rest of the ingredients until the mix is smooth.
2. Put the mixture into your ice cream maker and freeze it according to the directions on the box. For soft serve, you can eat it right out of the machine. For firmer ice cream, put it in the freezer for a few hours.

CREAMY FROZEN YOGURTS

11. VANILLA BEAN FROZEN YOGURT

Prep Time: 15 Minutes | Cook Time: 00 Minutes

Total Time: 15 Minutes | Serving: 8

Ingredients

- 1/2 vanilla bean
- 2 cups of plain
- 1 cup of heavy cream
- 1 pinch fine sea salt
- 1/2 cup of organic granulated cane sugar
- 2 Tbsps whiskey or vodka

Instructions

1. Over medium heat, mix the sugar, salt, vanilla pod scrapings, heavy cream, and vanilla until the mixture is hot and steamy. Stir the sugar into the cream to dissolve it. Cover and let it steep for 20 to 60 minutes so the vanilla can get into it.
2. Add the yogurt to a medium-sized bowl and use a whisk to make it smooth.
3. Pour the cream into the yogurt and mix it with a whisk. Add the whiskey and mix it in. It can be put in the fridge for up to two days or until cold.
4. Follow the maker's instructions for how to churn the yogurt mixture. Then, scrape it into a container, cover it, and put it in the fridge for at least two hours and up to a few weeks until it's firm.

12. CHOCOLATE GREEK YOGURT ICE CREAM

Prep Time: 20 Minutes | Cook Time: 00 Minutes

Total Time: 20 Minutes | Serving: 8

Ingredients

- 3 cups of greek yogurt
- 1 tbsp vanilla extract
- 1 cup of cacao powder
- Pinch of sea salt
- ½ cup of almond milk
- ⅔ cup of maple syrup

Instructions

1. Add all the ingredients to a blender and blend them well until the chocolate is well mixed and the mixture is smooth.
2. Put the mixture into an ice cream maker and churn it according to the directions that came with it. That's how long it takes for my ice cream maker to make this recipe. It will start to get thicker until it's like a soft serve. Over time, it will get a little firmer.
3. You can put it in ice cream bowls if you're making soft serve. If you like your ice cream thicker, scoop the frozen yogurt into a container that won't let air in or a pan lined with parchment paper. Seal the pan well with plastic wrap to avoid freezer burn. Put the jar in

the freezer for at least 30 minutes to make it firm. Let the frozen yogurt thaw a bit before you serve it. Add any toppings you want, and enjoy!

13. VANILLA FROZEN YOGURT WITH CHOCOLATE SWIRL

Prep Time: 15 Minutes | Cook Time: 30 Minutes

Total Time: 45 Minutes | Serving: 8

Ingredients

Ganache:

- 2 tbsp cocoa powder
- 1/4 tsp salt
- 3 tbsp honey
- 1 cup of full-fat coconut milk

For the frozen yogurt:

- 1/4 tsp salt
- 3/4 cup of honey
- Caviar from one vanilla bean
- 2 pounds full-fat plain Greek yogurt

Instructions

For the ganache:

1. Put everything in a small sauce pot and set it over medium-high heat. To stir, use a whisk. When the mixture starts to boil, turn it to a simmer immediately. Keep stirring the ganache for 10 minutes or until it has cut in half. Watch out for the ganache to not boil over.
2. Take it off the heat and put it in a mason jar made of glass. Put it in the fridge for at least two hours to cool down.

For the frozen yogurt base:

1. Mix everything in a big bowl by stirring it around. Put the dish in the fridge with the lid on for at least two hours to chill. Do the same thing with the container where you store frozen yogurt. Freeze it for at least 30 minutes to make it nice and cold.
2. Both of the mixtures should have been chilled for at least two hours. Then, follow the steps on your ice cream maker and put the yogurt mixture on the base. Let it churn for twenty to thirty minutes or until the ice cream is soft-serve-like.
3. Before you start the ice cream maker, take the ganache out of the fridge and let it return to room temperature. You could also heat it in the microwave for a few seconds to soften the ganache. Be careful not to heat it above room temperature, or the yogurt might melt.
4. When the yogurt is as smooth as a soft serve, put half of it into the container that has been kept cold. Add a tbsp or two of the chocolate ganache to the frozen yogurt. Mix the chocolate into the frozen yogurt with a butter knife. Place more ganache and the rest of the frozen yogurt on top. Make more swirl patterns with your butter knife.

14. HEALTHY RASPBERRY FROZEN YOGURT

Prep Time: 15 Minutes | Cook Time: 00 Minutes

Total Time: 15 Minutes | Serving: 6

Ingredients
- ⅓ cup of honey
- 10.6 ounce. frozen raspberries
- 1½ cup of plain Greek yogurt

Instructions
1. Put everything in a blender and blend until it's smooth and creamy. That's how long it should take.
2. The frozen yogurt is ready to be served; it will feel like a soft serve. If you want the texture to be firmer, put the mixture in a container, cover it, and freeze it for an hour or two. Every 20 minutes, stir it. It might need a few minutes to thaw after being fully frozen before you can scoop it up and serve it.
3. Use a blender to mix all the ingredients for ice cream until the ice cream is smooth and creamy. That's how long it should take. Put it in the fridge for an hour to cool down.
4. Once the mixture is cool, put it in your ice cream maker and freeze it according to the machine's directions.
5. Take the raspberry frozen yogurt out of the freezer and put it back in until you're ready to serve it.
6. Enjoy

15. LEMON FROZEN YOGURT

Prep Time: 20 Minutes | Cook Time: 00 Minutes

Total Time: 20 Minutes | Serving: 8

Ingredients
- 1/2 cup of fresh squeezed lemon juice
- zest of one lemon
- 1/4 cup of lite corn syrup
- 2 16 ounce whole milk Greek Yogurt
- 14 ounce sweetened milk
- 2 tsp vanilla

Instructions
1. Put the yogurt in a big bowl and use a whisk to make it smooth.
2. Mix the corn syrup, vanilla, and sweetened condensed milk with a whisk until smooth.
3. Blend the lemon zest and juice together with a whisk until the mixture is smooth.
4. Put it into a ready-to-use ice cream maker and churn it as directed.
5. Once the frozen yogurt is ready, you can serve it as is or with lemon zest.

16. LAVENDER FROZEN YOGURT

Prep Time: 25 Minutes | Cook Time: 00 Minutes

Total Time: 25 Minutes | Serving: 6

Ingredients

- ¼ tsp kosher salt
- 1 32-ounce BestSelf Plain
- 1 cup of sugar
- 1 tsp dried lavender
- 1 tsp vanilla extract

Instructions

1. For three hours, freeze the bowl of the ice cream maker before you use it.
2. In a large bowl, mix all of the ingredients well.
3. Put the food into the machine that makes ice cream. Make ice cream with an electric mixer or blender if you don't have one. Then freeze it.
4. For 35 to 40 minutes, mix. For soft serve, serve right away. For a firmer texture, freeze for 3–4 hours.

17. BERRY COCONUT FROZEN YOGURT

Prep Time: 15 Minutes | Cook Time: 10 Minutes

Total Time: 25 Minutes | Serving: 4

Ingredients

- ¾ cup of light coconut milk
- 4 ounces raspberries
- ¼ tsp kosher salt
- 2 tbsp coconut rum
- 8 ounces strawberries
- 2 tbsp raspberry jam
- ½ cup of plain Greek yogurt
- ¼ cup of shredded toasted coconut
- ¼ cup of honey

Instructions

1. Follow the steps to freeze the ice cream maker. Get the strawberry skin off and cut it into fourths. Put the chocolate, honey, jam, and coconut rum in a large bowl.
2. For an hour, leave the berries out in the open air to soften. Stir them around to coat them in the honey and rum.
3. Add the Greek yogurt, coconut milk, and salt to the bowl with the berries. Stir to mix. Put the mixture in a blender and blend or process it until smooth.
4. Put the mixture back in the bowl and cover it with plastic wrap so that it touches the top. Put it in the fridge for at least an hour to cool down.
5. Follow the steps on your ice cream maker to freeze it, and add the toasted coconut in the last 5 minutes of churning. Add more toasted coconut on top before serving.

18. PEACH AND PISTACHIO FROZEN YOGURT

Prep Time: 15 Minutes | Cook Time: 00 Minutes | Total Time: 15 Minutes | Serving: 8

Ingredients

- 1 tsp vanilla extract
- ½ tsp salt
- 4 Tbsp honey
- 1/3 cup of pistachios
- 4 Tbsp granulated sugar
- 3 large unpeeled peaches
- ½ cup of cream
- 2 cups of full-fat Greek yogurt

Instructions

1. Using pulses, break up the pistachios in the food processor. Stack them in a modest bowl. Save it for later.
2. Add the honey, sugar, and peach pieces to the food processor bowl. Mix it in a blender until it's smooth. Put the rest of the ingredients and blend until everything is well-mixed. Put the mix into a bowl. Fry the pistachios in a pan.
3. An ice cream maker is used to churn the mixture. If you don't have one, put the mixture in the freezer until it's almost set. If it's frozen, take it out and mix it well with a spatula. Do this two or three times, and then put the whole thing in the freezer to set.

19. MINT CHIP FROZEN YOGURT

Prep Time: 20 Minutes | Cook Time: 00 Minutes | Total Time: 20 Minutes | Serving: 6

Ingredients

- 2 cups of whole-milk Greek yogurt
- 1 cup of fresh mint leaves
- 2 ounces dark chocolate
- 1/2 tsp peppermint extract
- 1/2 cup of brown rice syrup
- 1 cup of heavy cream

Instructions

1. Cut the mint leaves into big chunks and add them to a pot with cream. Over medium heat, bring to a simmer. Stir and press the mint leaves occasionally to get the oils out. Add the brown rice syrup and mix it in when it starts to simmer. Then turn off the heat. Put the mix on the stove and let it steep for 30 minutes.
2. Using a fine-mesh sieve, strain the cream mixture into a bowl to remove the mint leaves. Put the yogurt and peppermint extract in the bowl and mix them with a whisk. Set the bowl in the fridge overnight for at least 30 minutes with the lid on top.
3. Use an ice cream maker and follow the directions on the box to churn the yogurt mixture. Add the chocolate to the yogurt after it's done churning. You can serve it immediately or put it in a container with a lid and freeze it. It will get firmer in the freezer over time.

20. MANGO LASSI FROZEN YOGURT

Prep Time: 35 Minutes | Cook Time: 00 Minutes

Total Time: 35 Minutes | Serving: 6

Ingredients
- 1/2 tsp cardamom
- 1 tsp vanilla extract
- 16 ounces Greek yogurt
- 2 mangoes
- 3 tsp yellow food coloring
- 1/2 cup of sugar

Instructions
1. To start, put two fresh mangoes in a blender with just enough water to make a smooth paste.
2. Use an ice cream maker to mix 16 ounces of Greek yogurt, the mango mixture, and 1/2 cup of sugar.
3. Add 1/2 tsp cardamom and 3 drops of yellow food colouring while the mixture is still moving in an ice cream maker to make it a bright yellow colour. Add half a tsp of vanilla extract, too.
4. If you churn the frozen mango lassi for 30 minutes, it will be ready to put in the freezer. Let it freeze for at least four hours before you serve it.

21. HONEY ALMOND FROZEN YOGURT

Prep Time: 10 Minutes | Cook Time: 20 Minutes

Total Time: 30 Minutes | Serving: 6

Ingredients
- 1 tsp almond extract
- 2 cups of plain yogurt
- 1/3 cup of sugar
- 2 cups of Greek Yogurt
- 1/3 cup of sliced almonds
- 5 tbsp honey

Instructions
1. Mix the two yogurts, sugar, and honey in a large bowl. Add the almonds and almond extract and mix them well.
2. Mix the yoghurt with an ice cream maker until it freezes and gets smooth. You can eat them or freeze them for a treat later.

GOURMET GELATOS

22. AUTHENTIC ITALIAN GELATO

Prep Time: 10 Minutes | Cook Time: 10 Minutes | Cooling Time 45 Minutes

Total Time: 1 Hour 5 Minutes | Serving:4

Ingredients

- lemon zest or vanilla extract
- 250 ml heavy cream
- 350 ml milk
- 4 egg yolks
- 150 g granulated sugar

Instructions

1. Wash the egg yolks and sugar at high speed for about five minutes until you get a soft, fluffy cream.
2. Put the milk in a pot and almost boil it. Put it in the oven for 5 minutes. One way to ensure the temperature stays at about 85°C is to use a kitchen thermometer.
3. Move the fluffy cream made of eggs and sugar to a saucepan. Slowly pour the hot milk. Mix it up as you go. Now is the time to add flavor to the gelato. You can use grated lemon zest or two drops of vanilla extract or vanilla bean. Now, turn the heat back up and cook for five more minutes.
4. Take it off the heat and add the cold heavy cream. Mix. You now have a lukewarm mix.
5. Put the basic mix into the ice cream maker and turn it on. Based on the model, it will take around 40 minutes. When the time is up, your gelato is ready!

23. DARK CHOCOLATE AND NUTELLA GELATO

Prep Time: 15 Minutes | Cook Time: 25 Minutes

Total Time: 40 Minutes | Serving: 6

Ingredients

- 1/2 cup of milk
- 3 egg yolks
- 7 ounce. baking chocolate callets
- 2 cups of whipping cream
- 1 cup of Nutella
- 2/3 cup of water
- 7 tbsp. sugar
- chocolate sauce:
- 4 ounce. baking chocolate callets
- 1/2 cup of whipping cream

Instructions

1. Bring the water and sugar to medium-high heat to make syrup, and do not stir for 5 to 7 minutes. It's done when the edges of the syrup turn golden.
2. Use a metal bowl to mix the egg yolks and beat them until they are thick, pale yellow, and creamy. Slowly put the syrup into the egg yolks while whisking them. The mixture will get creamier and have more volume. Keep whisking it until it gets cool. Then, make a reservation.
3. Carefully bring the cream to a boil in a pot.
4. Put the chocolate in a metal bowl after breaking it into small pieces.
5. Drop by drop, add the hot milk and cream to the chocolate. Let it sit for three minutes, then stir it until it melts. Let it cool.
6. Put the egg yolk mixture into the chocolate that has been cooled down.
7. Put it in the ice cream maker and do what it says on the box.
8. While the chocolate chips and cream are heating up in a small saucepan over low heat, stir them until the sauce is smooth. Put it on top of the ice cream and serve.

24. PISTACHIO STRACCIATELLA GELATO

Prep Time: 30 Minutes | Cook Time: 00 Minutes

Total Time: 30 Minutes | Serving: 8

Ingredients

- 7 ounces unsweetened pistachio paste
- 1 ½ cups of whole milk
- 1 ½ ounces single-origin dark chocolate
- ½ tsp grated lemon
- 4 large egg yolks
- ¾ cup of granulated sugar
- ½ tbsp refined coconut oil
- ⅛ tsp kosher salt
- 1 cup of heavy cream

Instructions

1. Mix milk, cream, and zest in a medium saucepan. Without stirring, cook on medium-low for 5 minutes until the mixture steams without bubbling. Stop cooking, cover, and infuse for 10 minutes.
2. Meanwhile, whisk egg yolks, sugar, and salt in a medium bowl until smooth. Reserve until use.
3. Pour infused milk through a fine wire-mesh strainer into another bowl; discard solids. Whisk infused milk into yolks slowly. Clean saucepan.
4. Return the milk-yolk mixture to a clean saucepan. Stir constantly with a wooden spoon over medium-low heat until the mixture is thick enough to coat the back of a spoon, 6 to 10 minutes, avoiding bubbles. Stop cooking. Using a fine wire mesh strainer, pour into a medium bowl and discard solids. Mix in pistachio paste. Put a medium-sized bowl in a large bowl of ice water and stir it every so often for 8 minutes or until the mixture reaches room temperature. Chill the mixture for 1 to 12 hours in a container that can be closed again.
5. Place chilled pistachio mixture in the ice cream maker's frozen freezer bowl and follow the manufacturer's instructions for soft-serve consistency.
6. On high power for one minute, stir the chocolate and oil around in a small bowl every 15 seconds. Give it 5 minutes to cool down. Save until you need it.
7. While the maker is running, slowly stream chocolate into soft-serve gelato until well combined, about 1 minute. Cover gelato with plastic wrap directly on the surface in an 8- x 4-inch loaf pan. Let freeze for 4 hours until firm. Gelato can be kept in the freezer for a week in a container without air. Put gelato in the fridge for about 40 minutes until it reaches 16°F or can be scooped.

25. SICILIAN-STYLE GELATO

Prep Time: 20 Minutes | Cook Time: 10 Minutes

Total Time: 30 Minutes | Serving: 8

Ingredients

- 1 cup of heavy cream
- 2 tbsp cornstarch
- 1 vanilla bean split lengthwise
- 2 cups of milk
- 1 large egg yolk
- ¾ cup of granulated sugar

Instructions

1. Pour 1 cup of milk and all the cream into a medium saucepan. Add the split vanilla bean if you are using it. Heat on medium until the edges bubble.
2. Mix 1 cup of milk, sugar, and cornstarch in a small bowl. Whisk cornstarch into the hot milk saucepan after removing it from the heat. Put the pan back on medium heat and stir the mixture for 6-8 minutes until the sugar melts and gets thicker.
3. In a medium bowl, whisk the egg yolk for 30 seconds to a minute or until it turns pale and thick. Slowly put a ladleful of the hot milk mixture to the egg yolk while whisking it all the time. Then, slowly pour the mixture into the saucepan while whisking it again.
4. Get off the heat. Pour into an airtight container. After cooling to room temperature, refrigerate for several hours or overnight.
5. Fish the vanilla bean from the custard and discard.
6. Strain Sicilian-style gelato base for the smoothest texture. Put into an ice cream maker and churn per the manufacturer's instructions. Turn off the machine when the gelato is thick and icy but spoonable.
7. Freeze the gelato for two hours in an airtight container.
8. Ice crystals will form after that, making the texture less smooth. Gelato can be eaten for two months, but I recommend eating it immediately.
9. Sicilian-style gelato is easier to scoop when brought to room temperature 20 minutes before serving. It will also let you enjoy the treat at its ideal temperature and texture.

26. RHUBARB GELATO

Prep Time: 25 Minutes | Cook Time: 00 Minutes

Total Time: 25 Minutes | Serving: 4

Ingredients

For the rhubarb compote:

- 1 pound young rhubarb stalks
- 3/4 cup of organic sugar
- 1 tbsp water

For the gelato:

- 1/4 cup of mascarpone
- 2" piece whole vanilla bean
- 2 1/2 cups of whole milk
- 1/3 cup of organic sugar
- 2 tbsp cornstarch

Instructions

1. Heat water, rhubarb, and sugar in a medium saucepan over medium-high heat to make compote. To dissolve sugar, stir. Slowly simmer rhubarb slices on medium heat for 5–6 minutes to release juice and break apart. Stir occasionally for even cooking. Move to a bowl to cool down to room temperature.
2. Put 2 cups of milk and the vanilla bean in a medium heavy-bottomed saucepan and boil. Stop cooking.
3. Mix the remaining 1/2 cup of milk, sugar, and cornstarch in a separate bowl. Stir the cornstarch into the hot milk and heat again. After boiling, reduce heat and simmer for 5–6 minutes, stirring constantly, until the mixture thickens.
4. Add vanilla bean seeds to the custard after removing the vanilla bean. Cool to room temperature in a bowl. Cover and refrigerate in the freezer for 2 hours or 45 minutes after cooling.
5. Whisk the mascarpone into chilled gelato until well blended. Put the custard in the ice cream maker and freeze according to the instructions. When the gelato is firm, add the rhubarb compote to the ice cream maker bowl and churn for 1 minute. Place in a container and freeze until serving.
6. Gelato can be frozen for two weeks, but it's best fresh. Remove from freezer and let soften for 15–20 minutes before serving.

27. VEGAN RASPBERRY ROSE GELATO

Prep Time: 20 Minutes | Cook Time: Minutes

Total Time: 20 Minutes | Serving: 4

Ingredients
- 1/2 cup of raw almond butter
- 1 15 ounce can full-fat coconut milk
- 3/4 cup of soft, pitted Medjool dates
- 1 1/2 cups of frozen or fresh raspberries
- 1 Tbsp rosewater
- 1 tsp pure vanilla extract

Instructions
1. Put everything in a blender and blend until it's smooth.
2. Put it in an ice cream maker and follow the directions on the machine. Put it in a bowl if you don't have an ice cream maker. Every half hour, stir it until it's the consistency of thick malt.
3. Put the mixture into a container that can go in the freezer and has a lid. Freeze it again until it's firm enough to scoop. Leave it out for 15 minutes before serving if it gets too hard.

28. VANILLA MILK GELATO

Prep Time: 10 Minutes | Cook Time: 10 Minutes

Total Time: 20 Minutes | Serving: 8

Ingredients
- 1 tsp pure vanilla extract
- 1 vanilla bean
- 1 cup of heavy cream
- 2 cups of whole milk
- 4 large egg yolks
- 3/4 cups of granulated sugar

Instructions
1. Place the vanilla bean and milk in a medium saucepan over medium heat. Stir the mixture every so often with a heat-safe spatula until it simmers. Mix the egg yolks and sugar well in a medium-sized bowl while you wait. Do this until the egg yolks lighten in colour.
2. Slowly put the hot milk into the egg yolks while the whisk continues. Scrub the bowl and pour everything back into the pot.
3. Put the pan back on the heat and use a heat-safe spatula to stir the mixture for about 3 to 4 minutes or until it gets thicker. Take the pan off the heat and throw away the vanilla bean. Be sure to mix in the vanilla extract and cream. Let it cool down.
4. Put the mix into an ice cream maker and follow the maker's instructions to make the gelato until it's frozen and easy to scoop. You could also freeze the mixture in a metal container, beating it every hour until it's easy to scoop.

29. EGGNOG GELATO

Prep Time: 30 Minutes | Cook Time: 30 Minutes

Total Time: 1 Hour | Serving: 8

Ingredients

- 1 cups of cream
- 2 cups of milk
- 5 yolks
- ½ cup of sugar
- ¾ tsp nutmeg
- 3 tbsp rum/bourbon

Instructions

1. Mix the egg yolks and sugar pale yellow with a whisk to make them pale yellow.
2. It's ready when the milk, cream, and nutmeg simmer.
3. Slowly put the milk and cream mixture into the egg and sugar mixture.
4. Bring it back to the saucepan and cook, stirring slowly and constantly, until it gets thick. It needs to reach 170°F.
5. Take it off the heat. Add the rum or bourbon and stir. Put it in the fridge for at least four hours and overnight.
6. Put your ice cream into your ice cream maker the next day. In about 20 minutes, it should be thick enough to eat like soft serve ice cream. After the last step, it will be more like ice cream. You will eat it as a soft serve now.
7. Put it in a container that can be frozen. Cover the container with parchment paper and freeze for at least 4 hours if the container has no lid.

30. MANGO GELATO

Prep Time: 20 Minutes | Cook Time: 00 Minutes | Churn: 30 Minutes

Total Time: 50 Minutes | Serving: 6

Ingredients

- 1/2 cup of cold water
- 2/3 cup of heavy cream
- 1/2 cup of granulated sugar
- 2 pounds very ripe mango
- 3 tbsp freshly squeezed lime

Instructions

1. Half-fill a big bowl or pot with ice water.
2. Bring the sugar & water to a boil in a medium-sized saucepan over medium-high heat, stirring occasionally. For two to three minutes, boil the syrup until the sugar is gone and it is clear.
3. Put the pan right into the ice water right away. Let it cool down, stirring now and then until the sugar syrup is at room temperature.
4. Take the pits out of the mangoes and peel and dice them. In a blender or food processor, blend or process the mango, lime, lemon juice, and sugar syrup until the mixture is smooth. Put the mix in a container & add the cream while stirring. Cover and put in the fridge for about three hours or until it is freezing.
5. For how long it takes to freeze the mixture in an ice cream maker, follow the steps that come with it. This should take about 20 to 30 minutes.
6. Put in a container that can be closed again, covered, and frozen for about two hours or until firm. Put the mix into bowls and serve.

31. COFFEE GELATO

Prep Time: 20 Minutes | Cook Time: 15 Minutes

Total Time: 35 Minutes | Serving: 4

Ingredients

- 1 shot of espresso
- 4 egg yolks
- 3/4 cup of sugar
- 2 1/2 cups of milk
- 1/2 cup of cream

Instructions

1. In a medium-sized bowl, whisk egg yolks and sugar together with a fork until the mixture doubles and turns yellow. Set aside.
2. Put the cream and milk in a medium-sized saucepan and set it over low to medium heat. Slowly stir the milk and cream with a spoon or whisk until foam forms around the edges.
3. Next, put the egg and sugar mix into the milk and cream in the saucepan. Stir the mixture repeatedly until it coats the back of a wooden spoon. Take a shot of cold espresso and add it. You can use a tbsp of instant coffee mixed with a tsp of water instead of espresso. Use a whisk to mix it all together slowly.
4. Through a sieve or fine strainer, pour the mix into a bowl. This will eliminate any solid egg bits and make the texture smoother and more even. Cover the gelato mixture and put it in the fridge for at least four hours or overnight.
5. Lastly, put the gelato mix into an ice cream maker and freeze it according to the machine's directions. Put the ice cream out of the machine or use a spoon to put it in a container. Cover it and freeze it.

VEGAN ICE CREAM

32. VEGAN COCONUT RASPBERRY ICE CREAM

Prep Time: 10 Minutes | Cook Time: 00 Minutes | Total Time: 10 Minutes | Serving: 6

Ingredients
- 1 cup of raspberries
- 1 tsp vanilla extract
- 2 13.66 ounce Thai coconut milk
- 3/4 cup of granulated sugar

Instructions
1. In a blender, mix the sugar, vanilla, and coconut milk. About 30 seconds of blending should do it.
2. Follow the directions that came with your ice cream maker to freeze. Add the raspberries in the last few minutes of churning. You will serve the ice cream immediately if you want a soft-serve texture. If you want a firmer texture, you can freeze it in a container.

33. VANILLA BEAN COCONUT ICE CREAM

Prep Time: 30 Minutes | Cook Time: 00 Minutes | Total Time: 30 Minutes | Serving: 8

Ingredients
- 2 14-ounce cans of coconut cream
- 1 vanilla bean pod
- 2 tsp pure vanilla extract
- 1/2 cup of organic cane sugar
- 1 pinch of sea salt

Instructions
1. Freeze your bowl to make ice cream the night or day before you use it to make it cold.
2. Put vanilla extract, scraped vanilla bean, organic cane sugar, sea salt, and coconut milk into a high-speed blender the next day. Blend high for one to two minutes until the mixture is completely creamy and smooth. This will help the sugar dissolve completely. If it's too sweet, add more cane sugar or agave. If it tastes too vanilla, add more vanilla.
3. Put the mixture right into an ice cream maker that has been chilled, and churn it for about 45 minutes, or as directed by the manufacturer. It needs to look like a soft serve.
4. Once the ice cream is smooth, put it in a large container that can go in the freezer and use a spoon to make the top even.
5. Put a tight lid on top and freeze for at least four to six hours or until firm. Leave out for 5 to 10 minutes before serving to soften. A hot ice cream scoop makes it easier to scoop.
6. It can be frozen for up to 10 days but tastes best when fresh. It goes well with pies, cakes, cookies, and other foods.

34. VEGAN MINT CHOCOLATE CHIP ICE CREAM

Prep Time: 20 Minutes | Cook Time: 00 Minutes

Total Time: 20 Minutes | Serving: 8

Ingredients

- 1/2 cup of mini chocolate chips
- 2 cans of full-fat coconut milk
- 1 cup of fresh spinach
- 1/4 cup of fresh mint leaves
- 3/4 cup of granulated sugar
- 1 tsp vanilla extract
- 1/8 tsp salt
- 1 tsp peppermint extract

Instructions

1. It's best to freeze the ice cream maker bowl the day before you want to make it. Fourteen hours of chilling time are needed.
2. Add mint leaves, sugar, peppermint extract, vanilla extract, and salt to a high-speed blender. Mix it for two to three minutes or until it's creamy and smooth.
3. Put the mix into the machine that makes ice cream. Follow the directions on the ice cream maker for how to churn. Add the mini chocolate chips in the last two to three minutes.
4. After that, move to a container that can go in the freezer. Freeze for at least 4 hours with the lid on. It's also possible to eat it right away as a soft serve.
5. Freeze the ice cream for a while. Allow to thaw for 5-10 minutes before using. Enjoy!

35. VEGAN CHOCOLATE CHERRY ICE CREAM

Prep Time: 30 Minutes | Cook Time: 25 Minutes

Total Time: 55 Minutes | Serving: 6

Ingredients

- 4 ounces chopped dark chocolate
- 1 tbsp cane sugar
- 1 tsp vanilla extract
- 3 1/3 cups of canned coconut milk
- 12 ounces pitted and halved cherries
- 1/4 tsp salt

Instructions

1. Add the ice cream freezer bowl in the freezer the night before you want to make ice cream.
2. Blend the coconut milk, 1/2 cup of sugar, vanilla, and salt in a blender for one minute. Put this mixture in a container in the fridge for an hour or up to two days.
3. Set the oven to 400F. Put the cherry halves on a baking sheet lined with parchment paper. Then, sprinkle the last tbsp of cane sugar on top of them. Put the cherries in the oven for 10 minutes. Mix them on the sheet. Roast them for 10 to 15 minutes or until soft and shriveled but still juicy. Let it cool down so the cherries are ready to eat. Cut the cherries pretty small on the baking sheet to use in your ice cream.
4. Get your machine ready to make ice cream. Mix in the coconut milk that has been cooled. Do what the directions say for your ice cream maker. Add dark chocolate and cherries to the machine when the ice cream is almost done. The ice cream will get a little runnier momentarily, but the machine will quickly make it smooth again. You will also finish churning the ice cream, pour it into the loaf pan, and add the mix-ins by hand, ensuring they are fully mixed with a spatula.
5. Freeze the ice cream for 30 to 60 minutes or until you like how it feels. Enjoy it with scoops or on a cone.

36. VEGAN PISTACHIO ICE CREAM

Prep Time: 40 Minutes | Cook Time: 00 Minutes

Total Time: 40 Minutes | Serving: 8

Ingredients

- 60 ml almond milk
- 200 g pistachios
- 400 g chilled full-fat canned coconut milk
- 1 tsp almond extract
- 60 g coconut oil
- pinch sea salt
- 2 tsp vanilla extract
- 180 ml pure maple syrup
- 30 g pistachios

Instructions

1. Put the pistachios in a large bowl, cover them with water, and put them in the fridge overnight or for at least 4 hours. You can also quickly soak them in boiling water for 30 minutes to an hour.
2. Clean the pistachios and peel off as many skins as possible. You should be able to easily peel them off with your fingers because the water will have made them loose.
3. Blend it all on high speed until it's smooth and creamy, with no lumps.
4. Put the mixture into the ice cream maker and churn it as the machine directs.
5. Put the ice cream in a container that won't let air in, top it with chopped pistachios, and freeze for 4 hours.
6. Let it thaw for 10 minutes before you serve it. Before you use it, warm up your ice cream scoop in hot water.
7. If you store this vegan pistachio ice cream in a container without air, it will last for a couple of months.

37. VEGAN CHAI ICE CREAM

Prep Time: 30 Minutes | Cook Time: 00 Minutes

Total Time: 30 Minutes | Serving: 6

Ingredients

- 1/4 cup of agave nectar or maple syrup
- 1/4 cup of cane sugar
- 1 1/2 cups of raw cashews
- 1/4 tsp each black pepper
- 1 tsp pure vanilla extract
- 3 packets of chai tea
- 1/4 cup of coconut oil
- 1/2 tsp each cinnamon and ginger powder
- 1 cup of light coconut milk

Instructions

1. Freeze your churning bowl overnight to make it cold in the morning. Also, soak your cashews the night before or for at least four to six hours before you blend them.
2. Make the ice cream after waiting at least 10 minutes. Bring 3/4 cup of water to a boil and add your chai tea. It needs to be very strong. Squeeze out any extra tea from the tea bags, then put the cups in the fridge to cool down.
3. While you wait, drain the cashews and get the other ingredients ready.
4. Use Liquify and put the tea and other ingredients into a blender if you can. Blend until the mixture is creamy and smooth, which should take 3–4 minutes. Taste it and add or take away sugar or flavorings as needed.
5. Put the mixture in your chilled ice cream maker bowl. Churn the mix according to the manufacturer's directions for about 45 minutes or until it is freezing. It should look like a thick, soft serve.
6. Put it in a container that can go in the freezer, cover it, and freeze it until it's hard. This should take at least 6 hours, but ideally overnight. This food can be frozen for up to a week.

38. AVOCADO ICE CREAM

Prep Time: 10 Minutes | Cook Time: 00 Minutes

Total Time: 10 Minutes | Serving: 6

Ingredients

- 3 Avocados ripened
- ¾ cup of Granulated Sugar
- 1 tbsp Fresh Lime Juice
- ¼ tsp Kosher Salt
- 1 cup of Reduced Fat Plain Greek Yogurt
- 8 ounces Bittersweet Chocolate
- ½ cup of Heavy Cream

Instructions

1. Cut the avocados in half and take out the pits. Using a spoon, put chunks of the insides into a food processor. Heavy cream, sugar, lime juice, and salt should be added. It will take about two minutes of pureeing until the mixture is smooth and the sugar is gone.
2. Follow the directions on your ice cream maker for how to freeze it. Add the chopped chocolate 10 minutes before the time is up and mix. You can serve it immediately or freeze it in a container that won't let air in for up to 4 hours to make it firmer.
3. What you mix will get very firm after 4 hours. Rest on the counter for 15-20 minutes before serving.

39. VEGAN COFFEE ICE CREAM

Prep Time: 30 Minutes | Cook Time: 00 Minutes

Total Time: 30 Minutes | Serving: 6

Ingredients

- 1 cup of plant-based milk
- 1 ½ cups of raw cashews
- ¾ cup of white sugar
- ½ cup of espresso
- 1 tsp vanilla extract

Instructions

Softening the cashews:

1. Putting the cashews in warm water first helps them mix. If you have a strong blender, you can skip this step. If not, you need to do it to get ice cream that is smooth & creamy. Put the cashews in a small pot with water and cover them. Boil for about 10 minutes or until the cashews are very soft. Before you use cashews, drain and rinse them.

To make the ice cream:

1. Follow the directions that came with your ice cream maker to get it ready. I enjoy making ice cream with my Cuisinart machine.

2. Add sugar, espresso or coffee, cashews, plant-based milk, and vanilla to your blender. Stop the blender & scrape the sides if you need to until the mixture is smooth and creamy. Make sure that there are no chunks of cashews left in the mix.
3. Whirl the ice cream for about 25 minutes or until it's smooth, like a soft serve. Put the ice cream in a container that you can seal and freeze for two hours or overnight until it gets firm. You can eat it right away. Scoop it up and enjoy! You can freeze dairy-free ice cream left over for up to two weeks in a safe container for freezing.

40. VEGAN BUTTER PECAN ICE CREAM

Prep Time: 15 Minutes | Cook Time: 00 Minutes

Total Time: 15 Minutes | Serving: 10

Ingredients

Ice Cream:

- 2 cans of full-fat coconut milk
- 1 cup of packed dates
- 1 tsp vanilla
- 2 tbsp butter-flavored coconut oil
- ¼ tsp salt

Pecans:

- ¼ tsp salt
- ¾ cup of chopped raw pecans
- 1 tbsp butter flavored coconut oil

Instructions

1. Put the dates and one can of coconut milk in a small pan. Bring to a boil while stirring, often over medium-low heat.
2. Put the mixture in a high-powered blender after taking it off the heat. Mix in the vanilla, salt, and coconut oil until smooth. You can add the second can of coconut milk and blend it again. Mix the things until the mixture is smooth. The mixture should be put in a large glass dish with a lid in the fridge for at least 4 hours or overnight to cool down completely.
3. Come up with the pecans. Combine the pecans, coconut oil, and salt in a large skillet. 3–4 minutes on medium heat. It should be taken off the heat and put in a bowl until it is time to use.
4. Separately wrap a loaf pan in parchment paper and set it aside.
5. Put the cool mixture into your ice cream maker and churn it according to the manufacturer's instructions. It took 12 minutes. After three minutes, add the pecans. Put it in the freezer after you're done churning it. You can also eat it right away for a soft-serve texture.
6. For easier scooping, let it sit at room temperature for 10 minutes after taking it out of the freezer.

41. VEGAN CINNAMON ICE CREAM

Prep Time: 25 Minutes | Cook Time: 00 Minutes

Total Time: 25 Minutes | Serving: 4

Ingredients

- 1/4 tsp ground ginger spice
- 2 tbsp cornstarch
- 13.5 ounce of full-fat canned coconut milk
- 1/4 cup of maple syrup
- 2 tsp vanilla extract
- 2 1/2 tsp ground cinnamon
- 1/4 tsp fine sea salt
- 2 tbsp coconut sugar

Instructions

Cashew version:

1. You can make this one without corn. If you don't have a powerful blender, soak the cashews in warm water for a few hours, then drain and rinse them. Put everything into a blender and blend it until it's completely smooth. Put the mixture into your ice cream maker and churn it for 20 to 25 minutes, or until it turns into soft serve. Freeze for a few hours or until it's firm and easy to scoop.

Version with Cornstarch version:

1. Put everything in a small pot over medium-low heat except the vanilla. Whisk the mixture well until there are no more lumps.
2. Before it starts to boil, turn off the heat and whisk it all the time for one minute. Take it off the heat and add the vanilla while whisking.
3. Run the mixture through a fine mesh strainer to get rid of any lumps. Then, put it in a plastic container that won't let air in and put it in the fridge for at least two hours.
4. Once it's cool, either whisk it to make it smooth or strain it again. To make ice cream, put this in and wait for the magic to happen. It took about 25 minutes for mine. After being stirred in the ice cream machine, it will have a soft serve consistency. Put it back in the freezer for a few hours to get it to the consistency you want. If it freezes all the way through, let it sit out for a few minutes to soften up before you serve it. To get rid of it best, use an ice cream scooper.

FRUITY FAVORITES

42. PEACH ICE CREAM

Prep Time: 20 Minutes | Cook Time: 00 Minutes

Total Time: 20 Minutes | Serving: 4

Ingredients

- 2 cups of heavy cream
- 1/2 tsp vanilla extract
- 1 cup of whole milk
- 1 1/4 cups of Granulated sugar
- 2 cups of chopped peaches

Instructions

1. Mix the chopped peaches with 1/2 cup of sugar in a medium-sized bowl. Let it sit for about 15 minutes so the peach pieces can release their juices.
2. Use a blender or food processor to make peaches smooth.
3. Mix the peach with the heavy cream, whole milk, vanilla extract, and the last 3/4 cup of sugar in a large bowl. Set aside.
4. Start the ice cream maker and get the freezer bowl out. Pour the peach mix into the ice cream maker that is already running. Following the manufacturer's instructions, let it run.
5. Now is the time for soft-serve ice cream.
6. Cover the peach ice cream with plastic wrap and put it in a bread loaf pan. This will make ice cream that can be scooped. Freeze for at least six hours or overnight. After that, serve the scoop.

43. STRAWBERRY ICE CREAM

Prep Time: 15 Minutes | Cook Time: 00 Minutes

Total Time: 15 Minutes | Serving: 12

Ingredients

- 1 cup of sugar
- 1 cup of whole milk
- 2 cups of chopped strawberries
- 2 cups of heavy cream
- 1 dash salt
- 1/2 tsp vanilla extract

Instructions

1. For the best results, freeze the bowl of a 2QT ice cream maker overnight.
2. Strawberry chunks and 1/2 cup of sugar should be mixed in a medium-sized bowl. Set aside 15 minutes to let the strawberries' juices come out.
3. Make strawberry juice in a blender or food processor.
4. Mix the strawberry mixture with the heavy cream, whole milk, vanilla extract, salt, and sugar in a large bowl. Set aside.

5. Pour the strawberry cream mixture into an ice cream maker set-up. Follow the manufacturer's instructions and let it run.
6. Now is the time for soft-serve ice cream.
7. Put ice cream into a bread loaf pan and cover it with plastic wrap. This will make ice cream that can be scooped. Freeze for at least six hours or overnight.

44. PASSION FRUIT ICE CREAM

Prep Time: 30 Minutes | Cook Time: 10 Minutes

Total Time: 40 Minutes | Serving: 6

Ingredients

- 1 tbsp vanilla extract
- 6 egg yolks
- Fresh passion fruit pulp to garnish
- 1 1/2 cup of heavy cream
- 3/4 cup of whole milk
- 3/4 cup of passion fruit puree
- 1 cup of granulated sugar

Instructions

1. Put sugar and egg yolks in a bowl and mix them. Mix the eggs and sugar with a hand mixer until the colour is light yellow.
2. Put the milk and 1/2 cup of heavy cream in a saucepan and set it over medium-low heat. Add the water and stir it around until it begins to boil. Don't let it boil. Slowly stir the hot milk and heavy cream into the egg and sugar mix. When you put the pan back on the stove, the custard should be hot and thick, about 165°. Keep the custard from getting too hot.
3. Take the custard off the heat. Use a mesh strainer to eliminate any egg bits that may have formed. Put the custard base in a container that won't let air in. Put it in the fridge until it's cold, preferably overnight.
4. Once the custard base is ready, mix the heavy cream, passion fruit puree, and vanilla extract. Then, pour the mixture into your ice cream maker and follow the directions that come with it.
5. Put the ice cream into a pan about the size of a loaf. Put it in plastic wrap and put it in the freezer until it freezes solid. Put ice cream into bowls and top with fresh passion fruit pulp to serve.

45. LEMON BLUEBERRY CHEESECAKE ICE CREAM

Prep Time: 20 Minutes | Cook Time: 00 Minutes

Total Time: 20 Minutes | Serving: 6

Ingredients

Berry Mixture:

- 1/4 cup of sugar
- 1 1/2 cups of blueberries

Ice Cream Base:

- 8 ounce cream cheese
- 1 Tbsp lemon juice
- 1 cup of sugar
- 2 cups of cream
- 1 cup of milk
- 4 squares of graham crackers
- 1 tsp vanilla
- 1 tsp lemon zest

Instructions

1. Blueberries and sugar should be boiled in a small saucepan until the blueberries burst and the mixture thickens. Allow to cool completely and set.
2. Mix sugar and cream cheese until they are smooth. Add the milk, vanilla, lemon juice, and zest, and beat well. Put in the fridge for a few hours or until it gets cold. A machine that makes ice cream.
3. Save half a cup of the blueberry sauce.
4. Put ice cream base, sauce, and graham cracker pieces in a container that can go in the freezer. Add spoonfuls of each of the ingredients in layers. Swirl slowly if you want to.
5. For two to three hours, or until hard, cover and freeze. If you want, serve with the blueberry sauce that you saved.

46. HEALTHY BLOOD ORANGE ICE CREAM

Prep Time: 40 Minutes | Cook Time: 00 Minutes

Total Time: 40 Minutes | Serving: 8

Ingredients

- 16 ounce Half and Half
- 32 ounce Plain
- 1 cup of Blood Orange Juice
- ½ tbs Xanthan Gum
- ⅔ cup of Truvia Spoonable
- 1 tbs Blood Orange Zest

Instructions

1. Put your ice cream maker bowl in the freezer for at least 24 hours.
2. Put the yogurt, half-and-half, and Truvia in a blender. Mix until it's smooth.
3. Blend again after adding the blood orange juice and zest.
4. Last, add the xanthan gum and blend it in until it's completely smooth.
5. Switch on the stand mixer and the "stir" speed. Attach the ice cream maker. Put the "batter" for the ice cream into the bowl and mix it around.
6. Put the mixture in a container that can go in the freezer, cover it, and freeze it until it has the texture you want. Put it in bowls and serve!

47. BLACKBERRY ICE CREAM

Prep Time: 15 Minutes | Cook Time: 00 Minutes

Total Time: 15 Minutes | Serving: 4

Ingredients

- 1 pint fresh blackberries
- ½ cup of white sugar
- ½ cup of whole milk
- 2 cups of heavy cream
- 1 tsp vanilla extract
- ½ tsp lemon zest

Instructions

1. Put blackberries, sugar, and lemon zest in the bowl of a food processor. Pulse the food until the mixture is smooth. Let it sit for a while.
2. Put the mixture through a fine mesh sieve and throw away the seeds. Put the puree back into the food processor. Mix in the milk, cream, and vanilla extract. For about 30 seconds, pulse the mixture until it is whipped.
3. Put the mixture into an ice cream maker and freeze it for about 20 minutes, or as directed by the manufacturer. Put in a container that won't let air in and freeze for two hours overnight until it's firm.

48. BANANA BERRY ICE CREAM

Prep Time: 20 Minutes | Cook Time: 00 Minutes

Total Time: 20 Minutes | Serving: 6

Ingredients
- 2 cups of whole milk
- 3 cups of sugar
- 6 cups of berries
- 4 cups of heavy cream
- 3 ripe bananas
- 3 oranges
- 3 lemons

Instructions
1. Add the first five things to a blender or the bowl of a food processor with a metal blade. Blend the orange juice and bananas first, then add the sugar, berries, and lemon juice.
2. Put everything above into a big bowl. Slowly add the cream, then the milk. Put the mix in the fridge and let it chill until it's cold.
3. Put the whole thing into a 6-quart ice cream maker and freeze it according to the manufacturer's directions.

49. WATERMELON MINT ICE CREAM

Prep Time: 1 Hour 30 Minutes | Cook Time: 30 Minute

Total Time: 2 Hour| Serving: 16

Ingredients
- 1 cup of heavy cream
- 2 cups of fresh mint leaves
- 1 cup of white sugar
- 4 egg yolks
- 1 cup of heavy cream
- 8 cups of watermelon chunks

Instructions
1. Blend the watermelon chunks using a blender or food processor until they are smooth. Strain the juices to get rid of any solids that are left, and set the juices aside.
2. In a saucepan, warm up one cup of heavy cream and the sugar over medium-low heat. Add the mint leaves to the warm cream and mix them in. Take the saucepan off the heat and cover it. Let it sit at room temperature for an hour to steep. Drain into a bowl, and then throw away the mint leaves.
3. Using a whisk, beat the egg yolks slowly in a bowl. Slowly pour the cream with mint into the egg yolks while whisking to keep the egg from cooking. Scrape the mixture back into the saucepan and set it over medium-low heat. While cooking, scrape the bottom of the pan often to keep stirring the mixture. Keep stirring until it thickens and coats the spatula. Pour the mixture through a strainer into a bowl with 1 cup of heavy cream. The watermelon juice should be mixed into the cream.
4. Pour into an ice cream maker and freeze according to the machine's directions.

50. FRESH BLUEBERRY ICE CREAM

Prep Time: 10 Minutes | Cook Time: 10 Minutes

Total Time: 20 Minutes | Serving: 8

Ingredients

- pinch of salt
- 2 cups of whipping cream
- 1 cup of whole milk
- 1 Tbsp vanilla
- 4 cups of fresh or frozen blueberries
- 2 cups of sugar
- 1 cup of half and half

Instructions

1. Make blueberries smooth in a blender.
2. Put sugar and pureed blueberries in a saucepan. Stir and heat until the sugar melts.
3. Cool the mixture in the fridge.
4. Mix the salt, vanilla, milk, 1/2 and 1/2, and cream. Mix.
5. Put it in the ice cream maker and churn it.
6. Put ice cream in the freezer to set up and get ripe.

51. COCONUT-PINEAPPLE ICE CREAM

Prep Time: 10 Minutes | Cook Time: 00 Minutes

Total Time: 10 Minutes | Serving: 8

Ingredients

- ½ cup of pineapple juice
- ½ cup of coconut flakes
- 1 cup of half-and-half
- ¾ cup of finely chopped fresh pineapple
- 1 tsp coconut extract
- 1 can sweetened cream of coconut

Instructions

1. Mix pumpkin puree, pineapple juice, coconut flakes, cream of coconut, and coconut extract in a big bowl.
2. Follow the maker's instructions and put the mixture into an ice cream maker. Process it until it gets thick. Put the mix in a container that won't let air in for about three hours or until it's firm.

KID-FRIENDLY FLAVORS

52. CINNAMON TOAST CRUNCH ICE CREAM

Prep Time: 30 Minutes | Cook Time: 00 Minutes

Total Time: 30 Minutes | Serving: 16

Ingredients

- 3 cups of Cinnamon Toast Crunch cereal
- 1½ cups of whole milk
- extra cereal for garnish
- 1/4 cup of brown sugar
- 1½ cups of half & half
- 2 cups of whipping cream
- 1½ Tbsp pure vanilla
- 1 cup of sugar
- 1 tsp cinnamon
- ¼ tsp salt

Instructions

1. For 30 to 45 minutes, let 2 cups of cereal soak in 1 1/2 cups of whole milk.
2. Get rid of the soggy cereal and strain the milk from the cereal.
3. Mix the milk with cereal, sugar, cinnamon, salt, half-and-half, vanilla, and whipping cream to make ice cream.
4. Follow the directions on the package.
5. Sprinkle brown sugar on the last cup of cereal while the ice cream is churning. To melt the sugar, stir the cereal and brown sugar in a pan over medium-low heat. Melted sugar should be mixed into the cereal.
6. Give it time to cool down on a plate. Split up.
7. Before putting the ice cream in a container to freeze, mix the sugared cereal into it.
8. For extra fun, you can top the dish with extra cereal before serving.

53. CIRCUS ANIMAL COOKIE ICE CREAM

Prep Time: 20 Minutes | Cook Time: 10 Minutes

Total Time: 30 Minutes | Serving: 8

Ingredients
- 1 tsp vanilla extract
- ½ cup of granulated sugar
- 1 cup of whole milk
- 2 cups of heavy whipping cream
- 6 large egg yolks
- 1 tsp nonpareil sprinkle
- ½ cup of pink frosting
- 1 cup of circus animal cookies
- pinch of salt

Instructions
1. Spread the heavy whipping cream, milk, sugar, and salt out in a pot with a heavy bottom. Slowly warm them up until they begin to bubble.
2. While the cream mixture gets hot, whisk the egg yolks in a large bowl. With the whisk running the whole time, slowly add a cup of milk after the cream bubbles. Combine the egg yolks and add them to the pot and the cream.
3. Put it all in a pan and stir it slowly until it gets thick enough to coat the back of a spoon.
4. The custard should be poured into a large bowl through a fine mesh strainer. Vanilla should be mixed in. Once it's completely cold, cover it and put it in the fridge.
5. As directed by the manufacturer, churn in an ice cream maker.
6. Fastly mix in the cookies after the food has frozen. Make a few swirls in the frosting with a rubber spatula after adding it. This should be separate from the ice cream. The frosting should be swirly.
7. Fill a container in the freezer with about ⅓ of the ice cream. Use half of the sprinkles to cover the ingredients. Then add the rest of the sprinkles and another ⅓ of the ice cream. Place in the freezer and top with the rest of the ice cream.

54. COTTON CANDY ICE CREAM

Prep Time: 10 Minutes | Cook Time: 20 Minutes

Total Time: 30 Minutes | Serving: 8

Ingredients
- 3/4 White Sugar
- 1/2 Cup of Cotton Candy Syrup
- Wilton's Pink Food Coloring Gel
- 2 Cups of Heavy whipping Cream
- 1 Cup of Whole Milk
- 1 tsp. Vanilla Extract

Instructions
1. Mix milk and sugar together in a bowl until there is no more sugar.
2. Then, put in the heavy cream and vanilla.
3. Put in cotton candy syrup
4. Colour the food pink with gel

5. Mix well
6. Pour into ice cream maker after mixing well. I make ice cream with a Cuisinart.
7. Twenty minutes from now, the ice cream will be ready.
8. You can put the freezer bowl back in the freezer to give it more time to harden after it's done.
9. Serve right away if you like your ice cream softer.
10. Put it in a bowl or cone.
11. Have fun!

55. RAINBOW SHERBERT

Prep Time: 10 Minutes | Cook Time: 20 Minutes

Total Time: 30 Minutes | Serving: 10

Ingredients
- 1 ½ cups of sugar
- 2 cups of milk
- 2 cups of heavy whipping cream
- 12 ounces raspberries
- ½ cup of lime juice
- orange and green food coloring
- 1 cup of orange juice

Instructions
1. Put the milk, cream, and sugar in a small pot. Heat them over medium to high heat for 5 to 8 minutes or until the sugar is gone. If you put it in the freezer for 20 minutes, it will get cold quickly.
2. Using a blender, blend the raspberries until they are smooth. Take the puree and strain out the seeds.
3. To freeze the milk base, use an ice cream maker and do what it says on the box.
4. Once it's frozen, divide the mixture into three bowls. Add raspberries to one, lime juice to another, and orange juice to the last bowl. You can add food colouring to the orange and lime now to make the colour stand out more.
5. Dollop each flavour however you'd like into a container that can go in the freezer. Do not mix them up. Put it in the freezer until it gets solid. Each ice cream maker has its instructions for how long to do this. This ice cream is a little firmer than soft serve because my machine makes it thick. In about an hour, it will be ready. You might need more time to freeze.

56. VANILLA ICE CREAM

Prep Time: 5 Minutes | Cook Time: 00 Minutes

Total Time: 5 Minutes | Serving: 6

Ingredients
- 1 Tbsp of vanilla extract
- 1 ¾ cups of heavy whipping cream
- ⅛ tsp salt
- 1 ¼ cup of whole milk
- ¾ cup of granulated sugar

Instructions
1. Mix everything in a big bowl with a whisk.
2. Put it in an ice cream maker and churn it the way the maker's directions say to.
3. Once the churning is done, pour the mixture into a container that won't let air in and can go in the freezer. Freeze it for at least 12 hours before serving.

57. FRUITY PEBBLES ICE CREAM

Prep Time: 40 Minutes | Cook Time: 10 Minutes

Total Time: 50 Minutes | Serving: 10

Ingredients
- 2 ½ cups of Fruity Pebbles cereal
- ½ cup of white granulated sugar
- 2 tbsp whole milk
- 2 tbsp light corn syrup
- 1 ½ tbsp cornstarch
- 2 cups of whole milk
- 1 ¼ cups of heavy cream
- ½ tsp kosher salt
- 2 tsp vanilla extract

Instructions
1. Combine 2 cups of milk, cream, sugar, corn syrup, and salt in a heavy-bottomed kettle with 5 quarts. Get it boiling over medium-high heat.
2. Make a cornstarch slurry by whisking the last 2 tbsp of milk and cornstarch together while the mixture is heating.
3. Boil the milk mixture for two minutes. Add the cornstarch slurry slowly while whisking the mixture. Back to the heat, and stir constantly for about 30 seconds until the mixture gets thicker.
4. After thickening the mixture, remove the heat and mix in the vanilla extract and Fruity Pebbles. Then, let it cool down to room temperature.
5. Make sure there is no extra liquid in the cereal before putting it in an airtight container. Place in the fridge for at least eight hours.
6. According to the manufacturer's instructions, freeze in an ice cream maker once it's been chilled. Mine takes 25 minutes.
7. In a container that won't let air in, put it in the freezer for 4 to 6 hours.

58. BIRTHDAY CAKE ICE CREAM

Prep Time: 5 Minutes | Cook Time: 20 Minutes

Total Time: 25 Minutes | Serving: 6

Ingredients

- 1/2 Cup of Rainbow Sprinkle Jimmies
- 2 Bakery Cup of cakes with Vanilla Frosting
- 1 tsp Pure Vanilla Extract
- 1 1/2 Cups of Half and Half
- 1 1/2 Cups of Heavy Cream
- 1 tsp Pure Almond Extract
- 1 Cup of Granulated Sugar

Instructions

1. Whisk the heavy cream, half-and-half, and sugar in a large bowl.
2. Mix it up until the sugar is gone.
3. Pure almond and vanilla extract should be added.
4. Make ice cream by putting the mix into the machine.
5. Cut or crumble both cup of cakes into small pieces and set them aside.
6. Turn it on and wait twenty to twenty-five minutes.
7. Add the cup of cake crumbs and sprinkles once it has started to get firm and almost frozen. Two more minutes of mixing.
8. Leave the ice cream maker off and pour the ice cream into a medium-sized bowl. Let it freeze for 4 hours before you serve it.

59. CANDY CANE ICE CREAM

Prep Time: 10 Minutes | Cook Time: 00 Minutes

Total Time: 10 Minutes | Serving: 8

Ingredients

- ¾ cup of crushed candy canes
- ½ tsp peppermint extract
- 1½ cups of heavy cream
- 2 tsp vanilla extract
- ⅛ tsp kosher salt
- ½ cup of sugar
- 1½ cups of milk

Add-Ins:

- 1 cup of peppermint bark
- ¼ cup of additional crushed candy canes
- ⅓ cup of cold chocolate sauce

Instructions

1. Pulse the milk and candy together in a food processor or blender until the candy is mostly mixed.

2. Put the sugar, vanilla, peppermint extract, and salt in a bowl and whisk them together. Add the peppermint candy mix to the milk. Put it in your ice cream maker and follow the directions that come with it.
3. Put a third of the churned ice cream into a freezer container that won't let air in. Add pieces of candy cane and chocolate sauce on top if you want. Use chopped peppermint bark as a topping. Add two more layers.
4. You can serve soft-serve ice cream immediately or freeze it until it gets hard.

60. CARAMEL CORN ICE CREAM

Prep Time: 20 Minutes | Cook Time: 25 Minutes

Total Time: 45 Minutes | Serving: 4

Ingredients
- 1 cup of raw corn kernels
- 2 Tbsp Brown Butter
- 3 cups of eggless ice cream base
- ½ tsp sea salt
- ¾ cup of whole milk
- 2 Tbsp granulated sugar
- 2 tbsp Caramel Sauce

Instructions
1. Using medium-low heat, melt the brown butter in a small pot. This is what will give the corn its flavour. Two minutes of stirring after adding the corn kernels. Put the milk, sugar, and salt in and raise the heat to medium-high. Continue to boil. Cover the pot on low heat and wait 25 minutes. Cook for 5 minutes and stir the food.
2. Use a hand-stick blender to blend the corn mixture. Then, strain it through a fine-mesh strainer into a container, pressing on the blended mixture to get as much liquid as possible. Throw away the solid mix. Once the liquid is at room temperature, put it in the fridge to get cold. Before using, scrape off the top of the butter that has hardened.
3. Mix the ice cream base and corn flavouring with a bowl whisk.
4. For ice cream, put the mix in and turn it on. Mix it up and churn it until it feels like soft-serve ice cream. Add two tbsp of the caramel sauce before you turn off the machine. Cut it off when you're done mixing.
5. Put layers of the mixture and thick swirls of the vanilla caramel sauce into containers that can go in the freezer one after the other.
6. Place parchment paper over the ice cream and press it down so it sticks. After that, put a lid on top. What matters is that the parchment doesn't go over the edge. A minimum of 6 hours in the coldest part of your freezer is needed to make it firm. For up to three months, it will last.

61. BUBBLE GUM ICE CREAM

Prep Time: 30 Minutes | Cook Time: 12 Minutes

Total Time: 42 Minutes | Serving: 10

Ingredients

- 10 pieces pink bubble gum Dubble Bubble
- 1-2 drops red food coloring
- 3/4 cup of granulated sugar
- 1 cup of small gumballs
- Pinch salt
- 2 1/2 cups of half & half
- 1 1/2 cups of heavy cream
- 1 tsp vanilla extract
- 2 egg yolks

Instructions

1. Over medium heat, whisk together everything but the gums. Make sure there are no lumps in the egg yolks.
2. Bring to a light boil after adding the pink bubble gum pieces. Work the base with a whisk until it gets thicker and the gum softens.
3. Cover it off the heat, and put it in the fridge until it's cold. It takes at least three hours, but it's best to leave it overnight.
4. To get rid of the gum, strain the ice cream base through a paper towel in a colander before putting it into the frozen bowl of an ice cream maker.
5. Start an ice cream maker and put the base in it. Churn it for 20 to 30 minutes.
6. Put the gumballs in after the food is frozen. Eat it immediately, or put it in a container that won't let air in and freeze it.

DREAMY CHOCOLATE DELIGHTS

62. HEALTHY CHOCOLATE ICE CREAM

Prep Time: 25 Minutes | Cook Time: 00 Minutes

Total Time: 25 Minutes | Serving: 5

Ingredients

- 1 tsp vanilla extract
- 1 cup of plain nonfat Greek yoghurt
- ¼ tsp salt
- ½ tsp xanthan gum
- ½ cup of unsweetened cocoa powder
- 1 ½ tsp liquid stevia
- 1 ¼ cups of milk

Instructions

1. Put an electric ice cream maker's bowl in the freezer the night before you want to make ice cream. Lay it out to freeze for 12 to 16 hours.
2. Combine everything in a big bowl. Assemble using an electric mixer for one minute or until very foamy.
3. Carefully take the bowl from the ice cream maker out of the freezer. Putting it on the ice cream maker, connecting the lid and paddle, and then turning it on. As the ice cream maker is turning, add the milk mixture. Your ice cream should be frozen and consistent after 15 to 20 minutes of churning in the ice cream maker. Right away, serving gives the best texture and taste.

63. DARK CHOCOLATE FUDGE ICE CREAM

Prep Time: 20 Minutes | Cook Time: 00 Minutes

Total Time: 20 Minutes | Serving: 3

Ingredients

- 1 tsp powdered instant coffee
- 2 2/3 cups of heavy cream
- 1 cup of sugar
- 1 pinch salt
- 2 ounces semisweet chocolate
- 1 1/3 cups of milk
- 3 ounces unsweetened chocolate
- 1 vanilla bean

Instructions

1. Melt the chocolate and coffee powder in a double broiler over hot water that is not simmering.
2. Heat the cream, milk, sugar, salt, and vanilla beans in a heavy saucepan until hot.
3. Be sure to stir to break up the sugar.
4. Mix the chocolate in until it's smooth after adding it.
5. Take the vanilla bean and cut it in half down the middle. Then, put the seeds into the chocolate cream.

6. Throw away the pod.
7. Put the chocolate cream on ice or in the fridge to cool it down completely.
8. Following the directions that came with your ice cream maker, freeze it.

64. MINT CHOCOLATE CHIP ICE CREAM

Prep Time: 40 Minutes | Cook Time: 00 Minutes

Total Time: 40 Minutes | Serving: 8

Ingredients

- 5 drops of green food coloring
- ½ tsp pure mint extract
- 2 tsp vanilla extract
- large pinch salt
- 1 cup of milk
- 4 ounces bittersweet chocolate
- 14 ounce can of sweetened condensed milk
- 2 cups of heavy cream

Instructions

1. Put all the ingredients in a large bowl except for the chocolate. Use a whisk to mix them well. Put the mixture into your ice cream maker and follow the directions on the box.
2. Use 50% power to melt the chocolate five minutes before the churning is over. As the machine works, slowly pour the chocolate into it.
3. The ice cream and chocolate will harden and crack at different temperatures. This will make delicious chocolate chips. It's called stracciatella.
4. Place the ice cream in a container that can go in the freezer. Freeze it until it's hard, which should take about an hour.

65. CHOCOLATE HAZELNUT ICE CREAM

Prep Time: 45 Minutes | Cook Time: 30 Minutes

Total Time: 1 Hour 15 Minutes | Serving: 8

Ingredients

Homemade Hazelnut Butter:

- 1 cup of raw hazelnuts

Ice Cream Base:

- 2 ounces of semisweet chocolate
- ½ tsp pure vanilla extract
- 1 tbsp unsalted butter
- batch of homemade hazelnut butter
- 1½ cups of heavy cream
- small pinch of kosher salt
- 6 egg yolks
- ¾ cup of granulated sugar
- 1½ cups of whole milk

Instructions

1. For the homemade hazelnut butter, Preheat the oven to 350°F. Use silicone baking mats or parchment paper to line a sheet pan. It will take 10 to 15 minutes of toasting for the raw hazelnuts to get fragrant and for the skins to start cracking.
2. Move the hot hazelnuts to the middle of a large, clean kitchen towel. After closing the towel around the hazelnuts, let them cool for 5 to 10 minutes. Take hazelnuts out of their shells by rolling and rubbing them in the towel with your hands. If necessary, toast any hazelnuts that won't come off their skins in the oven for 3 to 5 minutes.
3. Put the hazelnuts in the bowl of a large food processor. Processing for 3 to 5 minutes, scraping down the bowl's sides with a spatula every few minutes or until a very smooth and creamy butter forms. It will be dry, thick, and crumbly within the first few minutes of processing. The hazelnut oil will escape, turning the mixture into a loose nut butter. Set this aside while you make the base for the ice cream.
4. Gather the ingredients for the ice cream base: Whisk the egg yolks and granulated sugar together in a medium-sized bowl until the mixture is thick and pale yellow. Whole milk and heavy cream should be added while whisking. Put the mixture in a medium-sized pot. Using a wooden spoon to stir the mixture often and adjusting the heat as needed, put it over medium-low heat until it has thickened. It's ready when the mixture sticks to the back of the spoon and coats it. Immediately put the ice cream mix into a large mixing bowl. Combine the hazelnut butter, salt, and vanilla extract and mix them completely with a whisk. Relax until it's room temperature. Using a fine-mesh sieve, strain the mixture into a large container that can go in the fridge. Wrap it up and put it in the fridge until it's very cold, ideally for 12 hours.
5. Please make sure you follow the directions for your ice cream maker. Are you almost done making the ice cream? Put the chocolate and butter in a small bowl that can go in the microwave. Put the chocolate and butter in the microwave and melt them together.

Stir the mixture every 15 seconds until it is smooth. Before you seal a small plastic bag, press out any extra air. During this whole process, the chocolate should be warm.
6. To quickly pour the chocolate into the ice cream while it's still churning, cut a small hole in the middle corner of the plastic bag. Before putting the ice cream in an airtight container, covering the top with butcher paper or plastic wrap is best. At least four to six hours in the freezer will make sure the ice cream is completely frozen.

66. CHERRY CHOCOLATE CHUNK ICE CREAM

Prep Time: 15 Minutes | Cook Time: 10 Minutes

Total Time: 25 Minutes | Serving: 12

Ingredients

- 2 cups of heavy cream
- 1 cup of granulated sugar
- 5 large egg yolks
- 2 cups of whole milk
- 3/4 cup of dark chocolate chunks
- 1 1/2 cups of pitted cherries

Instructions

1. Mix the milk, cream, and 3/4 cup of sugar in a large pot. Bring the mix to a boil slowly and stir it with a whisk until there is no more sugar. Lower the heat.
2. Mix the egg yolks and the rest of the sugar in a small bowl. Adding a whisking motion will make it a little thicker and lighter in colour. Slowly add 1/4 cup of the milk mixture, and whisk the eggs. Stir the egg mix well after adding a quarter cup of milk.
3. Set up an ice bath in a big bowl and put a medium bowl in it. Cover the bowl with a fine mesh strainer.
4. Add the cream mixture to a big pot. Over medium-low heat, stir the custard and use a heat-safe spatula to scrape the bottom and sides of the pan until it gets thick enough to stick to a spoon. Pour the custard into the bowl through a strainer. Stay inside until it is cooler.
5. Put the custard in the fridge overnight or until it's cold.
6. For an electric ice cream maker, put the custard in the freezer can and freeze it as the machine tells you to. When the ice cream is soft-serve-like, add the chocolate chunks and cherries. Mix it up. Move to a container that won't let air in and freeze.

67. CHOCOLATE ORANGE ICE CREAM

Prep Time: 50 Minutes | Cook Time: 00 Minutes

Total Time: 50 Minutes | Serving: 6

Ingredients
- 1 1/2 tsp Food Grade Orange Oil
- 1 cup of cashews
- 1/2 cup of maple syrup
- 3/4 cup of cocoa powder
- 1 can full-fat coconut milk

Instructions
1. Put the cashews and everything else into a high-speed blender like this one. For about one minute, blend at medium to high speed. Clean the bowl's sides, then blend for 15 seconds or until smooth.
2. Put the ice cream base in an ice cream maker and churn it according to the maker's directions. This should take thirty to forty minutes.
3. Cover the ice cream as a soft serve if you want to eat it, and move it to a loaf tin or another freezer-safe container. Freeze it for a couple more hours until it's more solid.
4. The ice cream should be left at room temperature for 10 minutes before being served. In a week, enjoy.

68. STRAWBERRY CHOCOLATE SWIRL ICE CREAM

Prep Time: 20 Minutes | Cook Time: 00 Minutes

Total Time: 20 Minutes | Serving: 4

Ingredients
- 1 can of coconut milk
- 1 1/2 cups of fresh strawberries
- 1/4 cup of dark chocolate
- 3 tbsp pure maple syrup

Instructions
1. Take off the green tops of the strawberries and set 5 of them aside. After you add the rest of the strawberries, coconut milk, and honey, blend or process the food. Mix until it's smooth.
2. Cut the last five strawberries into small pieces and add them to the strawberry mix.
3. Cut the chocolate into small pieces or melt it to make chocolate ribbons.
4. Use an ice cream maker and put the strawberry mix in it. Let it work for 10 minutes. Put the ice cream maker on and slowly pour the melted chocolate or chocolate chunks while the machine runs. Run it for another 15 to 20 minutes. Pack it up and freeze it if you plan to eat it later.
5. If you want it a little softer, let it thaw for 5-10 minutes before serving.

69. DARK CHOCOLATE ICE CREAM

Prep Time: 10 Minutes | Cook Time: 15 Minutes

Total Time: 25 Minutes | Serving: 4

Ingredients

- 1 cup of whole milk
- 1/3 cup of dutch process cocoa powder
- 8 ounce bittersweet chocolate
- 1 tsp vanilla extract
- 1/4 tsp salt
- 2 cups of heavy cream
- 4 egg yolks
- 3/4 cup of granulated sugar

Instructions

1. In a saucepan, stir the cocoa powder, sugar, and salt. To keep the cocoa powder from sticking together, whisk it well. Little by little, add the milk and heavy cream while whisking. Lower the heat a bit. Stir it all the time and bring it to a low boil. Take it off the heat.
2. Spoon the egg yolks into a small bowl after beating them. Mix ½ cup of the hot liquid into the egg yolks slowly. Slowly put the egg yolks back into the saucepan while stirring. Put the chocolate chips and mix them in.
3. Put the pan on low heat. It will get thick after 5 to 7 minutes of cooking on low heat. Do not boil. An instant-read thermometer should show 170°F.
4. Take it off the heat. Add the vanilla extract and mix well.
5. Put the chocolate mix through a sieve and into a big bowl. Set the big bowl with the chocolate mix on an ice bath. The chocolate mixture should be stirred a lot until it reaches room temperature. Cover it and put it in the fridge for 4 hours or up to a day once it's at room temperature.
6. Take the chocolate mix out of the fridge. Put it into an ice cream maker and freeze it according to the machine's directions. When you're done churning, serve the ice cream immediately because it will be thick. This is great to eat right after churning. You can put the ice cream in a container that won't let air in, cover it, and freeze it until you're ready to serve it. This will make the ice cream hard.

70. CHOCOLATE FUDGE BROWNIE ICE CREAM

Prep Time: 40 Minutes | Cook Time: Minutes | Chill Time: 2 Hours

Total Time: 2 Hours 40 Minutes | Serving: 12

Ingredients

- 300 ml double cream
- 140 g gooey chocolate fudge brownie
- 300 ml whole milk
- 120 g caster sugar
- 4 large egg yolks UK large
- 200 g good quality dark chocolate

Instructions

1. Put the brownie in the fridge ahead of time to make it a little firmer. This will make it easier to cut into small pieces.
2. Add the sugar and egg yolks to a large bowl that can handle heat. Stir the ingredients together until they are smooth and fully mixed.
3. Put the milk and broken chocolate into a large pot.
4. Mix the milk and chocolate over low to medium heat and stir until completely melted.
5. Take it off the heat and stir until it cools for a few minutes.
6. Pour the warm chocolate milk slowly onto the egg-sugar mixture while beating it with a wooden or silicone spoon all the way through until it is well mixed.
7. The chocolate mix should be put back into the pan. Stir the mixture often while the heat is low to medium. Once it starts to steam, it will get a little thicker, like custard. Make the mix almost boil, but don't let it go over.
8. Take it off the heat and add the cream right away. Thoroughly mix everything.
9. Pour the chocolate batter through a sieve into jugs or a big bowl to eliminate any lumps.
10. Leave the batter alone to cool down as quickly as possible.
11. Put it in the fridge for about an hour after it's cool.
12. Once it's completely cold, use an ice cream maker to make ice cream according to the directions that came with it.
13. Cut the brownies into small pieces that are easy to eat while the batter is mixed.
14. Take the paddle from the ice cream maker and add the brownie pieces to the mix before putting the ice cream in a container.
15. Add the brownie chunks and mix them in so they are spread out evenly.
16. Put the mixture into a container that won't let air in and freeze until it's completely hard.

71. CHERRY CHOCOLATE CHIP ICE CREAM

Prep Time: 40 Minutes | Cook Time: Minutes | Chill Time: 5 Hours

Total Time: 5 Hours 40 Minutes | Serving: 8

Ingredients

- 1/8 cup of honey
- 2 cups of heavy whipping cream
- 1 cup of whole milk
- 1/2 cup of fresh Bing cherries
- 2 large eggs
- 1/2 cup of pure maple syrup
- 1/2 cup of granulated sugar
- 5 ounce mini semisweet chocolate chips

Instructions

1. Mix sugar, honey, and maple syrup in a small saucepan over medium-low heat. The sugar should be completely dissolved before you add the cherries. Keep cooking for 5 to 10 minutes until the syrup gets thicker and the fruit has added flavour and a nice glaze to the cherries.
2. After taking it off the heat, strain it and set the syrup aside. Set the cherries and syrup aside to cool, and then put them in separate bowls in the fridge to cool down.
3. Whisk the eggs in a bowl for one to two minutes until they are light and fluffy. Gradually whisk in the chilled syrup mixture, and then keep whisking for another minute or so until everything is well mixed.
4. Combine the cream and milk and mix them with a whisk.
5. Place the mixture in a container that can go in the freezer, cover it, and freeze it for 20 minutes.
6. After the mixture has cooled, put it in your ice cream maker and freeze it as the machine tells you to.
7. As an alternative to making ice cream, if you don't have one, try Five minutes of mixing with a hand mixer. If your freezer is cold, put it back in there for another 20 minutes or up to three hours. Perform this step three or four times until the ice cream is thick and smooth.
8. When the mix is stiff and airy, add the chocolate and cherries and keep churning or mixing until everything is well combined. You can serve it immediately like soft serve or put it back in the freezer for another two to four hours until it gets firm.
9. Let it thaw on the counter for a few minutes before serving if you can't get your scoop in.

ADULT FRIENDLY

72. BAILEYS ICE CREAM

Prep Time: 10 Minutes | Cook Time: 20 Minutes Chill Time: 4 Hours

Total Time: 4 Hours 50 Minutes | Serving: 8

Ingredients

- 2 cups of heavy cream
- 5 tbsp Baileys Irish cream
- 1 tbsp vanilla extract
- 2 cups of whole milk
- 1 cup of sugar
- 7 egg yolks

Instructions

1. Mix the sugar, whole milk, and heavy cream in a saucepan using a whisk. On medium-low heat, bring to a boil. Keep whisking every so often to help the sugar dissolve. Stop cooking it when it starts to simmer. Not boiling can make the milk separate.
2. About three minutes of whisking in a bowl will make the egg yolks and vanilla light.
3. Add about ¼ to ½ cup of the warm cream to the egg mixture as you keep whisking. This makes the eggs runny, so they cook slowly. This needs to be said several times.
4. Re-add the egg-cream mixture that has been cooled down. Bring back to a simmer while whisking all the time over medium-low heat. Stay away from boiling. About six to ten minutes, or until the mixture gets thick enough to cover the back of a wooden spoon. Activate the heat.
5. Put it in a big bowl for mixing. Wait a few minutes for the custard to cool down, then put plastic wrap on it. Put in the fridge until it's cold. For best results, leave it there for at least four hours, but I like to leave it overnight to be sure it's really cold.
6. Pour custard into an ice cream maker and churn it according to the directions that came with the machine. Pour in the Baileys in the last few minutes of churning. Please wait to do this. If you don't, the alcohol could mess up the freezing process.
7. Place in a container that won't let air in and freeze for a few hours. Happy eating!

73. TEQUILA LIME ICE CREAM

Prep Time: 15 Minutes | Cook Time: 30 Minutes

Total Time: 45 Minutes | Serving: 4

Ingredients

- 60 ml lime juice
- grated zest of 2 limes
- 150 g caster sugar
- 2 tbsp white tequila
- 200 ml double cream
- 400 ml coconut milk

Instructions

1. Put the cream, sugar, lime zest, and coconut milk in a medium-sized saucepan. Then, slowly heat the mixture. Mix the mixture occasionally until the sugar is gone and just about to boil.
2. Take it off the heat and add the lime juice while stirring. Put the mixture into a bowl, cover it, and put it in the fridge overnight to cool down.
3. Take the creamy mixture the next day and put it into an ice cream maker. Churn it for 15 minutes.
4. While the ice cream is still moving, slowly add the tequila. Keep churning it for another 15 minutes until it gets thicker and more like a soft serve.
5. Put the ice cream in a container that can go in the freezer and leave it there overnight to set.

74. AMARETTO ICE CREAM

Prep Time: 10 Minutes | Cook Time: Minutes | Chill Time: 2 Hours 20 Minutes

Total Time: 2 Hours 30 Minutes | Serving: 12

Ingredients

- 5 tbsp almond-flavored liqueur
- 2 cups of heavy whipping cream
- 1 cup of half-and-half
- ¾ cup of white sugar
- 1 tsp vanilla extract

Instructions

1. Mix sugar, heavy cream, and half-and-half in a big bowl until the sugar is gone. Put in the liqueur and vanilla and mix it well.
2. Put the mixture into an ice cream maker and freeze it according to the machine's directions until it's the consistency of "soft serve." Put it in a container that won't let air in and freeze it for about two hours before serving.

75. RED WINE ICE CREAM

Prep Time: 20 Minutes | Cook Time: Minutes

Total Time: 20 Minutes | Serving: 2

Ingredients
- 1/2 cup of milk
- 1/2 cup of dry red wine
- 1 cup of heavy cream
- 1/2 cup of sugar

Instructions
1. Put the milk, sugar, cream, and red wine in a medium bowl and stir until they are well-mixed.
2. If you want to make ice cream, follow the directions on your machine.
3. Churn until it gets thick and creamy. It took me about 15 to 20 minutes.

76. WHITE RUSSIAN ICE CREAM

Prep Time: 5 Minutes | Cook Time: 20 Minutes

Total Time: 25 Minutes | Serving: 4

Ingredients
- 1 cup of whole milk
- 2 1/2 Tbsp coffee liqueur
- Pinch of salt
- 1/4 cup + 1 Tbsp granulated sugar
- 3/4 tsp vanilla extract
- 2 Tbsp vodka
- 2 cups of heavy cream
- 7 egg yolks

Instructions
1. Mix the heavy cream, milk, one tbsp of sugar, and a pinch of salt in a medium-sized saucepan. On medium heat, cook the mix until it starts to boil.
2. Put the eggs and 1/4 cup of sugar in a huge bowl and use a whisk to mix them. Slowly put about half a cup of the hot milk into the egg mix with a whisk. Add the milk mixture a quarter cup at a time and mix it all in. After that, put it back in the pot.
3. Mix it slowly over medium-low heat until it gets thick enough to stick to a metal spoon. Then, take it off the heat and mix in the vodka, coffee liqueur, and vanilla. If you don't want a film to form on top of the custard, ensure the plastic wrap touches the top when you cover it. Cool down completely.
4. Follow the directions in the ice cream maker's manual to add the custard mixture and churn it. Put it in the fridge for at least 6 to 8 hours before serving.

77. TRIPLE GINGERBREAD ICE CREAM

Prep Time: 25 Minutes | Cook Time: 10 Minutes | Chill Time: 8 Hours

Total Time: 8 Hours 35 Minutes | Serving: 1

Ingredients

- 2 cups of heavy cream
- 1 Tbsp chopped fresh ginger
- ¼ cup of molasses
- ¼ tsp salt
- ¾ cup of brown sugar
- 2 Tbsp whiskey
- 1 ½ tsp powdered ginger
- 5 whole cloves
- ¼ tsp nutmeg
- 15 small gingerbread cookies
- 1 cup of whole milk
- 6 large egg yolks
- 1 ½ tsp cinnamon

Instructions

1. Place the milk and 1 cup of heavy cream in a large saucepan and heat them over medium-low heat. Spice the pan with ground ginger, cinnamon, nutmeg, cloves, brown sugar, and salt. Warm the sugar up by stirring it around.
2. Take the mix off the heat and let it sit for an hour. Bring the mixture back to a simmer after steeping.
3. To make the egg yolks, whisk them in a medium-sized bowl that won't get hot. Mix the egg yolks with the hot milk, then slowly pour about half. This will make the eggs less runny. Add the rest of the milk to the saucepan and remix the egg and dairy.
4. Slow down the heat and stir until it gets thick enough to coat the back of a wooden spoon. While you don't want it to boil, you want it to be very close.
5. Make an ice bath by putting a medium-sized bowl into a large bowl full of ice. This will keep the mixture from getting too thick. Put the last cup of cream into the smaller bowl.
6. Ensure that the ginger and cloves don't get through as you strain the hot milk into the cream. Add the molasses and mix it in. Put the bowl in the fridge for at least 4 hours with plastic wrap on top of it so that it touches the crème fraîche.
7. Use an ice cream maker and follow the directions that come with it as soon as the mixture is cool. If you want to use it, add the whiskey while it operates. Fry up some gingerbread cookies and add them just before it's done.
8. Put the ice cream in a container that won't let air in, and freeze it for another 6 hours or more to make it thicker.
9. Put in bowls and top with gingerbread men.

78. RUM RAISIN ICE CREAM

Prep Time: 10 Minutes | Cook Time: 5 Minutes

Total Time: 15 Minutes | Serving: 12

Ingredients

- 1 cup of raisins
- 6 egg yolks
- 1 cup of sugar
- 2 cups of whole milk
- 2 cups of whipping cream
- 4 ounces dark or amber rum
- 1 tbsp pure vanilla extract

Instructions

1. Soak the raisins in the rum in a container that won't let air in for one night. If I use a mason jar, I can shake it often to ensure the raisins are mixed in well.
2. The milk and cream should be hot but not boiling. You can do this in the microwave or stove over medium heat.
3. To make the egg yolks and sugar fluffy, whisk them together in a medium-sized saucepan for about three minutes.
4. Keeping the whisk going, add a cup of the scalded milk to the egg yolk and stir. So the egg yolks don't cook and scramble, this makes them less strong. Mix another cup of well with the egg yolk mixture using a whisk. Last, add the rest of the cream and scaled milk and make sure it's well mixed in.
5. Warm the pan on medium heat and stir the mixture slowly and steadily for about 5 minutes or until it gets thicker. Now, you should be able to dip the wooden spoon in the custard and use your finger to make a clear line on the back of the spoon. If you boil it, the mixture might separate.
6. Taking it off the heat, add the vanilla extract and mix it in. Put the custard in the fridge for several hours or overnight to make it cold. I put it in the fridge overnight so the raisins can soak up the rum.
7. Cool the custard, stir it well and pour it into your ice cream maker. Run the machine for 20 to 30 minutes or until the ice cream thickens.
8. Move the ice cream quickly to a metal or glass bowl that has been chilled. Add the raisins that have been soaked in rum and any extra rum that they haven't absorbed.
9. Put it in a container that won't let air in and freeze it in the deep freezer or the coldest part of your fridge freezer. For a few hours or, better yet, overnight before serving.

79. COFFEE HEATH BAR ICE CREAM

Prep Time: 30 Minutes | Cook Time: Minutes | Chill Time: 3 Hours

Total Time: 3 Hours 30 Minutes | Serving: 4

Ingredients

- 1/2 tsp vanilla extract
- 2 1/2 cups of cream
- 4 egg yolks
- 1/2 tsp espresso powder
- Pinch of salt
- 1/3 cup of brown sugar
- 4 ounces of Heath bars
- 1 1/2 cups of milk
- 1/3 cup of white granulated sugar
- 2 tsp instant coffee granules

Instructions

1. Add the brown sugar, instant coffee, espresso powder (if using), vanilla, salt, and 1 1/2 cups of the cream to a medium-sized saucepan. Mix the ingredients. Heat the base until it starts to steam while you keep whisking.
2. In a small bowl, beat the egg yolks. When the base starts to steam, take 1/2 cup of out of the pan and add it to the egg yolks. Whisk right away. When you add the eggs to the hot milk and cream mixture in the next step, they won't curdle because of this step.
3. Once the yolk mixture is fully mixed in, add it back to the rest of the base. Heat the mixture until it reaches 170°F or until it coats the back of a spoon.
4. Immediately remove the heat and pour it through a fine mesh sieve. Add the last cup of cold cream and set it aside to chill for several hours or overnight.
5. To make health bars crumbly, hit them repeatedly with the back of a wooden spoon. Put pieces of the candy bar in a container and freeze them while you make the ice cream.
6. Put the base into an ice cream maker and churn it according to the directions with your ice cream maker. Take out the ice cream and mix in the pieces of the candy bar.

80. VANILLA BOURBON ICE CREAM

Prep Time: 20 Minutes | Cook Time: 20 Minutes

Total Time: 40 Minutes | Serving: 1

Ingredients

- Pinch of salt
- 1 tsp vanilla extract
- 1-1/2 cups of heavy cream
- 4 large egg yolks
- 1-1/2 cups of whole milk
- 3/4 cup of sugar
- 2 tbsp bourbon
- 1 vanilla bean

Instructions

1. Put the bowl in the freezer for at least 24 hours before using an ice cream maker that needs a frozen bowl.
2. Warm up 1 cup of milk, 1 cup of cream, sugar, and salt in a heavy-bottomed saucepan until hot but not boiling. This will make the ice cream base. The vanilla bean and its seeds should be mixed into the milk. The bean itself should then be added. Take the lid off for 30 to 60 minutes and let the vanilla soak into the milk mixture.
3. Add the last 1/2 cup of milk and 1/2 cup of cream to a bowl. Cover the bowl with a mesh strainer. You are going to strain the ice cream base into this bowl. The filter makes the ice cream very smooth, and the cold milk and cream stop the cooking so the custard doesn't get too done.
4. Add the egg yolks to a different bowl and whisk them. Pour the vanilla mixture back into the pot of hot water for a short time when it's hot again but not quite boiling. Add a little of the warm milk mixture to the eggs while stirring to temper the eggs. This will help keep them from getting confused.
5. Increase the amount of hot milk and stir it in again. While stirring, keep adding liquid to the eggs until you have added about a cup of liquid. Next, put the egg mix back into the pan.
6. Over medium-low heat, use a heat-safe spatula to stir the mixture until it thickens and covers the spatula. Sometimes, depending on the pot and stove, it only takes a few minutes.
7. Pour the custard into the bowl with the milk and cream through a strainer. If you need to cool the ice cream quickly, you can immediately put it in an ice bath. Otherwise, put it in the fridge for at least eight hours.
8. Put the vanilla extract and bourbon in when you're ready to churn. Mix it up nicely. Fix the mixture in your ice cream maker following the maker's instructions. Put the ice cream in the freezer for a few hours before you serve it so that it can get firm.

81. WHISKEY ICE CREAM

Prep Time: 15 Minutes | Cook Time: 00 Minutes

Total Time: 15 Minutes | Serving: 4

Ingredients

- ¼ cup of Irish whiskey
- 5 large egg yolks
- Toasted chopped pecans
- ¼ cup of granulated sugar
- ⅛ tsp kosher salt
- 2 cups of heavy cream
- 6 tbsp salted caramel sauce
- 1 tbsp pure vanilla extract
- ¾ cup of milk

Instructions

1. Warm the cream, milk, sugar, and salt in a big pot using medium-low heat. As the milk settles and small bubbles form around the edges, stir the mixture a lot. Keep away from boiling.
2. Put the egg yolks in a different large bowl and use a whisk to mix them. Slowly add half of the cream to the bowl with the egg yolks while stirring when the cream is hot.
3. Put the pan back on the stove and slowly pour the egg yolk-cream mixture into it while stirring. Over low heat, stir the mixture often and scrape the pan's bottom with a heat-safe spatula or wooden spoon until it gets thick enough to cover the spoon.
4. Take the pan off the heat and add the vanilla extract and whiskey.
5. Put the custard in a container with a mesh sieve on top of it. Cover and put in the fridge until it's completely cold, which should take overnight.
6. Follow the directions on your ice cream maker to churn the custard once it is completely cold.
7. When the ice cream is done churning, put a third of it in the bottom of a container that can go in the freezer. Add two tbsp of salted caramel sauce on top. It's time for the last third of the ice cream. First, add two more tbsp of caramel, then the last third of the ice cream. Spread the last two tbsp of caramel on top. Toss the caramel around with a butter knife or chopsticks, making sure to reach the edges.
8. Freeze for four hours or overnight to get firm. Put extra caramel and pecans on top of the big scoops of ice cream.

82. LEMON BASIL SORBET

Prep Time: 15 Minutes | Cook Time: 10 Minutes

Total Time: 25 Minutes | Serving: 8

Ingredients

- 2 whole lemons, zest, and juice
- 27 ounce canned coconut milk
- 1/2 cup of honey
- 1/2 ounce basil chopped

Instructions

1. Put everything into a pot and stir it around a lot as you bring it to a boil. Cool, lower the heat, and put it down! How do you use an ice cream maker if you have one? Only make ice cream if you have one. Include 3 cups of ice and 1/3 cup of salt in two gallon-sized bags. Place the sorbet mix into two quart-sized bags and tie them shut. Fill gallon bags with ice and seal quart-sized bags. Shake the bags for 6 to 7 minutes or until the sorbet is frozen. Put the mixture into a pan, freeze it, and stir it every 30 minutes until it's firm.

83. TANGERINE GELATO

Prep Time: 5 Minutes | Cook Time: 00 Minutes

Total Time: 5 Minutes | Serving: 8

Ingredients

- ¾ cup of sugar
- 2 cups of tangerine juice
- 2 cups of whole milk

Instructions

1. Put everything into your gelato or ice cream maker and mix it all. Then, wait for it to thicken and start to freeze.
2. Before you serve it, let the finished product freeze for at least 4 hours.

84. WATERMELON MINT SORBET

Prep Time: 15 Minutes | Cook Time: 00 Minutes

Total Time: 15 Minutes | Serving: 6

Ingredients

- 1 tsp raw sugar
- pinch sea salt
- 4 pounds of watermelon
- 1 tsp mint
- 3 tbsp white rum
- 3 limes

Instructions

1. Put chunks of watermelon, sugar, lime juice, and rum in a blender. Break up the watermelon.
2. When you add the mint, blend it until it's broken into pieces.
3. Put it in the fridge for 30 minutes.
4. Place the mixture into your ice cream maker and follow the directions that came with it.
5. Put it in a container that won't let air in and freeze it for a few hours. Then serve it. If you leave the sorbet in the freezer for over a few hours, it will freeze solid. Leave it on the counter for about 20 minutes or until you can scoop it up.

85. ORANGE THYME SORBET

Prep Time: 10 Minutes | Cook Time: 20 Minutes

Total Time: 30 Minutes | Serving: 4

Ingredients

- 2 tbsp fresh orange
- 1/2 cup of white granulated sugar
- 3 cups of freshly squeezed orange juice

Instructions

1. Place all three things in a saucepan and heat them over medium-low heat.
2. Once it starts to boil, boil the heat and let it cook for 5 to 10 minutes.
3. Get it off the heat and put it in a bowl that can handle heat.
4. Put in the fridge for four hours or overnight.
5. Put the mixture in an ice cream maker and follow the directions on the machine's box.
6. Put the mixture in a plastic container with a tight lid.
7. After 3 hours, put it in the freezer.
8. Simply scoop and serve. Add sprigs of thyme as a garnish.

86. MIXED BERRY SORBET

Prep Time: 25 Minutes | Cook Time: 00 Minutes

Total Time: 25 Minutes | Serving: 4

Ingredients
- ¼ cup of fresh lemon juice
- ⅓ cup of agave honey
- 6 cups of mixed berries

Instructions
1. Mix the berries and agave nectar, honey, or sugar in a medium bowl. The juices will come out if the berries sit for 15 minutes.
2. Mix the berries, their juices, and lemon juice in a blender. Blend the food until it's smooth.
3. Cover the bowl with a fine-mesh sieve. Add the berry puree and press the juices through the sieve. Throw out the solids that are still in the sieve. Put it in the fridge for 30 minutes.
4. Put berry puree into the ice cream maker and follow the maker's directions for making ice cream.
5. Put it in a container that won't let air in and freeze for at least three to four hours. Do it.

87. PINEAPPLE COCONUT SORBET

Prep Time: 20 Minutes | Cook Time: 00 Minutes

Total Time: 20 Minutes | Serving: 8

Ingredients
- 1 1/4 cups of pineapple juice
- 1 tbsp lime zest
- 1/4 cup of agave syrup
- Pinch salt
- 1 tsp grated ginger root
- 1 tbsp chopped lemongrass
- 3/4 cup of sugar
- 1 tbsp lime juice
- 1 15-ounce can lite coconut milk

Instructions
1. Mix sugar, agave syrup, ginger root, lime juice, zest, cilantro, and salt in a small saucepan. Mix them. Bring to a simmer and stir it occasionally until the sugar is gone. Put the coconut milk and mix it in.
2. Put the saucepan in a bowl of ice water or the fridge until cold to chill the sorbet base. Pour into an ice cream maker and follow the manufacturer's instructions for how to make ice cream. Put the sorbet in a container that can be sealed and freeze it until it gets firm. You can also eat it while it's still soft and creamy.

88. MANGO SORBET

Prep Time: 25 Minutes | Cook Time: 00 Minutes

Total Time: 25 Minutes | Serving: 6

Ingredients
- 1 cup of granulated sugar
- 1 tbsp lime juice
- 4 mangoes
- 1 cup of water

Instructions
1. Put each thing into a food processor. Pulse until it's smooth.
2. Place the mixture from the food processor into the ice cream machine.
3. Follow the manufacturer's instructions for your machine when you churn the mixture.
4. Put it in a container and freeze it for at least an hour or until it gets hard.

89. GRAPEFRUIT & HONEY SORBET

Prep Time: 30 Minutes | Cook Time: 00 Minutes

Total Time: 30 Minutes | Serving: 12

Ingredients
- 1/4 cup of chopped crystallized ginger
- 3/4 cup of honey
- 1 Tbsp pure vanilla extract
- 3 large grapefruit
- 1 Tbsp grapefruit zest
- Pinch of sea salt

Instructions
1. Get rid of the pith and seeds by peeling and slicing the grapefruit. Blend the ingredients with a high-speed blender or food processor until smooth.
2. Process the honey, salt, vanilla, and grapefruit zest until mixed. Put it in the fridge with the lid on for at least two hours.
3. Put the mix into your ice cream maker after it has been chilled. Follow the directions on the package to make the sorbet. Put the mixture in a container that can go in the freezer and freeze it until it has the texture you want. Spoon into bowls, and then sprinkle crystallized ginger on top.

90. RASPBERRY SHERBET

Prep Time: 25 Minutes | Cook Time: 00 Minutes

Total Time: 25 Minutes | Serving: 4

Ingredients
- 1 1/2 Cups of whole milk
- 3 Cups of frozen raspberries
- 3/4 Cups of granulated sugar
- 1 1/8 tsp lemon juice

Instructions
1. Thaw raspberries until they are soft. Put raspberries, sugar, and milk into a blender or food processor. Mix until completely smooth. Using a strainer over a large bowl, pour the mixture to remove the seeds. Get rid of the solids. Add lemon juice and mix well.
2. Fill the ice cream maker with the ingredients and mix for 25 minutes, or as the manufacturer directs.
3. Put the mixture in a container that can go in the freezer. Put the sherbet in the freezer for at least four hours or until it's your desired consistency.

91. COCONUT LIME SORBET

Prep Time: 10 Minutes | Cook Time: 15 Minutes

Total Time: 25 Minutes | Serving: 12

Ingredients
- 1 cup of granulated sugar
- 1 tbs lime zest
- 2 tins full fat coconut milk
- 1/2 cup of fresh lime juice

Instructions
1. Put coconut milk, sugar, and zest in a medium saucepan. Mix them over medium-low heat until the sugar melts.
2. Put it in a medium-sized bowl, add the lime juice, and put it in the fridge for at least two hours.
3. Put it in an ice cream maker and churn it according to the machine's directions.
4. Move the sorbet to a container that will stay cold. Keep it frozen for two more hours until it's firm enough to scoop.

HOLIDAY FLAVORS

92. HOT CHOCOLATE ICE CREAM WITH MARSHMALLOWS

Prep Time: 10 Minutes | Cook Time: 5 Minutes

Total Time: 15 Minutes | Serving: 8

Ingredients

- 1/2 cup of granulated sugar
- 2 Tbsp light corn syrup
- 1 tsp cornstarch
- 2 cups of whole milk
- 1/2 cup of sifted hot chocolate mix
- 1 1/4 cups of heavy cream
- 1/8 tsp salt
- 8 ounces mini marshmallows
- 3 ounces cream cheese

Instructions

1. Add 2 tbsp of milk to the cornstarch and mix them with a whisk in a small bowl.
2. Mix the salt and cream cheese in a bowl that can handle heat until smooth.
3. Add the heavy cream, sugar, corn syrup, and milk to a medium-sized saucepan. Use a whisk to mix the ingredients. Over medium-high heat, bring to a boil. Boil for 4 minutes, stirring now and then. Using a whisk, add the cornstarch mix. Bring it back to a boil and stir it all the time with a heat-safe spatula for about one minute or until it gets a little thicker.
4. Before adding the hot milk, mix it with the cream cheese until it's smooth. Put the dish in the fridge with the lid on for several hours or overnight to completely chill.
5. Get the marshmallows ready at the same time. Cut the marshmallows you make yourself into small pieces. Wrap a big cookie sheet in foil and grease it a little. Cover the pan with marshmallows all over. Use a kitchen torch or toast the bread under the broiler. Put it in the freezer for two hours.
6. Once it's cold enough, freeze it in your ice cream maker according to the directions that came with it. Fold the marshmallows when you put the churned ice cream in a freezer container. Make sure to freeze it.

93. GINGERBREAD ICE CREAM

Prep Time: 35 Minutes | Cook Time: 00 Minutes

Total Time: 35 Minutes | Serving: 6

Ingredients
- 2 Tbsp molasses
- 2 tsp ground ginger
- 1 cup of low-fat milk
- 1 tsp cinnamon
- 2/3 cup of sugar
- 1 cup of heavy cream
- 1/2 tsp allspice
- 1/4 tsp ground cloves
- 1/4 tsp freshly grated nutmeg

Instructions
1. Mix everything in a big bowl with a whisk. Stir long enough for the sugar to dissolve and the molasses to be fully mixed.
2. Put the mixture into an ice cream maker and follow the machine's directions. It takes me about 25 minutes to make ice cream.
3. Put the ice cream in a container, wrap it in plastic, and freeze it to make it hard. Do this before bed or at least 4 to 6 hours later.

94. GINGER MAPLE MISO ICE CREAM

Prep Time: 15 Minutes | Cook Time: 5 Minutes

Total Time: 20 Minutes | Serving: 8

Ingredients
- ¾ cup of crystallized ginger
- 1 tbsp pure vanilla
- 1-2 tbsp miso paste
- 2 tbsp tapioca starch
- ⅓ cup of maple syrup
- 2 cans full fat coconut milk

Instructions
1. Start with one tbsp of miso and add more if you like it more salty.
2. Mix ½ cup of coconut milk and 2 tbsp of tapioca starch in a small bowl using a whisk. Put away.
3. Put the remaining coconut milk in a saucepan on medium-low heat. Stir the mixture often as you bring it to a simmer and cook for five minutes.
4. Add the tapioca starch mix, maple syrup, and miso to the saucepan. Stir the mixture some more as it gets thicker. Take it off the heat and let it cool down.
5. Pour the ice cream mix into the maker and follow the manufacturer's instructions.
6. Cut the ginger crystals into small pieces while making the ice cream.
7. As the machine continues, add ½ cup of crystallized ginger pieces once the ice cream has formed.
8. Keep going for a few more minutes until the ginger is fully mixed in. Put in a container that can go in the freezer, top with the rest of the ginger crystals, and freeze.

95. PUMPKIN PIE ICE CREAM

Prep Time: 20 Minutes | Cook Time: 30 Minutes | Total Time: 50 Minutes | Serving: 6

Ingredients
- 1 1/2 cups of whole milk
- 1/2 cup of granulated sugar
- 6 graham crackers
- 1 tsp vanilla extract
- 1/2 cup of packed brown sugar
- 1 cup of pumpkin pie filling
- 1/4 tsp salt
- 1 cup of heavy whipping cream
- 1 1/2 cups of half and half

Instructions
1. Mix the sugars, salt, and vanilla into the pumpkin pie filling.
2. Mix in the half-and-half, milk, and whipped cream. Mix everything.
3. Put it in the ice cream maker and follow the directions.
4. When the ice cream is almost done, add broken cookies or crackers and process for a few more minutes to mix the cookies into the ice cream.
5. To set up, put the ice cream in an insulation container and in the freezer.

96. CHAI LATTE ICE CREAM

Prep Time: 15 Minutes | Cook Time: 30 Minutes | Total Time: 45 Minutes | Serving: 8

Ingredients
- 3/4 cup of honey
- 1 tsp vanilla extract
- 2 cup of heavy cream
- pinch of salt
- 5 bags of chai tea
- 5 egg yolks
- 2 cup of whole milk

Instructions
1. Melt the honey in a saucepan while stirring the milk, 1 cup of cream, vanilla, and salt.
2. Put the chai tea bags in the cream mixture after removing the heat.
3. Leave the tea bags out for half an hour and let the mixture steep. Then, take out the tea bags and throw them away. Cool the mixture for 15 minutes.
4. Whisk the 5 egg yolks together in a different bowl. Pour about a half cup of the cooled cream mixture into the egg yolks slowly while whisking them all the time. This will temper the yolks. Then, put the egg yolk mixture in the pot with the initial cream mixture.
5. When heated over low heat, a candy thermometer should read 170 to 175 degrees on the new mixture. That line you make with your finger across the back of the spoon should stay there if you mix the ingredients.
6. Setting up a strainer over a big bowl, pour the custard through it to eliminate any egg bits. Then, add the last cup of cream and mix it all.
7. You can either put the bowl in a bath of ice to cool it down faster or in the fridge until it's very cold.

8. Then, following the manufacturer's instructions, churn the ice cream in your maker. I used a Cuisinart ice cream maker. When it was done, I put it in a locking mason jar to freeze for two more hours.

97. RHUBARB ICE CREAM

Prep Time: 50 Minutes | Cook Time: 00 Minutes

Total Time: 50 Minutes | Serving: 8

Ingredients

Compote:

- 1 Tbsp lemon juice
- 1/4 cup of sugar
- 13 ounces chopped rhubarb

Custard:

- 2/3 cup of sugar
- 2 large egg yolks
- 2 cups of heavy cream
- 1 large egg
- 1 cup of whole milk
- 1 tsp vanilla extract

Instructions

1. Mix the rhubarb, sugar, lemon juice, and water in a medium saucepan. Then, set the pan over medium-low heat and bubble away. In a 15-minute cooking time, stir the rhubarb often so that some liquid evaporates and gets thick and soft. Watch out that it doesn't get too brown on the bottom of the pan.
2. After letting the compote cool down, blend it or process it in a food processor until it is completely smooth. Put in the fridge until cold.
3. Make the custard at the same time. Beat the egg, yolks, sugar, and milk together, being careful not to break up the eggs. Put the cream in a medium-sized saucepan with a heavy bottom. Heat it until it starts to steam and bubble around the edges. Put the hot cream into the egg mixture while whisking all the time. Put it back in the pan and stir it around constantly while heating it on medium. Do this until the mixture starts to thicken. Do not boil it.
4. Put the mix through a sieve, add the vanilla, and stir. Then, let it cool down. Put in the fridge until cold.
5. Blend the cold custard sauce and cold rhubarb well. Put it in your ice cream maker and churn it as it says to. Cover the soft ice cream with a lid and freeze it until it's firm enough to scoop.

98. PISTACHIO ICE CREAM

Prep Time: 15 Minutes | Cook Time: 25 Minutes

Total Time: 40 Minutes | Serving: 10

Ingredients

- ¾ cup of chopped pistachios
- ¾ cup of sugar
- 1 tsp vanilla
- 1 cup of shelled pistachios
- 1 cup of milk
- 2 cups of whipping cream

Instructions

1. Place the sugar and 1 cup of pistachios in a food processor. Whirl until the mixture is very fine. You should stir the sauce to ensure all the nuts are ground up.
2. Ground pistachios and milk should be put in a medium-sized saucepan.
3. Mix the mixture often over medium heat until it starts to boil.
4. Not in the heat anymore. Let it cool down.
5. Put it in the fridge and let it chill for about two hours until everyone is completely cool.
6. The vanilla and whipped cream should be mixed in.
7. Add the mix to the ice cream maker.
8. Mix for 20 to 25 minutes or as directed by the manufacturer.
9. When the ice cream is still moving, add chopped pistachios to it.
10. Mix for five more minutes. This tasty ice cream is sure to please!

99. APPLE CIDER SORBET

Prep Time: 10 Minutes | Cook Time: 30 Minutes

Total Time: 40 Minutes | Serving: 12

Ingredients

- 2 cups of granulated sugar
- 2 cups of water
- ¼ tsp ground cinnamon
- 1 ½ cups of apple cider

Instructions

1. In a small saucepan, mix the sugar and water. Cook over high heat until the sugar is gone. Let the simple syrup cool down.
2. Pour the cold apple cider, simple syrup, and cinnamon into an ice cream maker insert that is already set up. Churn for 30 minutes.
3. Spread the sorbet in a bowl, cover it, and freeze it for at least three hours or until it's easy to scoop.

100. CARDAMOM PLUM SORBET

Prep Time: 15 Minutes | Cook Time: 15 Minutes

Total Time: 30 Minutes | Serving: 12

Ingredients

Roasted Plums:

- 5 cardamom pods
- ¼ cup of sugar
- 1 pound plums
- 2 tbsp fresh lemon juice
- 1 vanilla bean pod

Cardamom Plum Sorbet:

- 5 cardamom pods
- 1 quantity of roasted plums
- 1 cup of sugar
- 1 ½ cups of water
- fresh plums for serving

Instructions

1. Warm the oven up to 375°F.
2. Cut aside sugar, lemon juice, cardamom pods, vanilla beans, and plums in a roasting dish. Make sure they are all in a single layer. After 30 minutes, they should be soft. Take it out of the oven and let it cool down.
3. Toss the pits out of the plum and the solids away. Keep the juices.
4. Heat the water, sugar, and cardamom pods in a small saucepan over medium-high heat. Stir the mixture a few times as it boils.
5. Once the sugar is gone, take the pan off the heat and let it sit for 10 minutes so the cardamom flavour can fill it up. The cardamom simple syrup needs to be strained.
6. Cranberries, cardamom syrup, and juices were put into a high-speed blender. Mix until completely smooth. Screen the mixture through a fine mesh sieve.
7. Put the mixture in a container that won't let air in and put it in the fridge for two hours.
8. Follow the manufacturer's instructions and put the mixture into your ice cream maker. Churn it until it freezes.
9. Put the sorbet in a container that won't let air in and freeze it for 6 hours or overnight.
10. If you want to serve the sorbet, scoop it into a bowl. Put fresh plums on top.

101. LEMON CUSTARD ICE CREAM

Prep Time: 15 Minutes | Cook Time: 11 Minutes

Total Time: 26 Minutes | Serving: 8

Ingredients

- 5 tsp lemon zest
- 6 egg yolks
- 1/8 tsp fine sea salt
- 3/4 cup of fresh lemon juice
- 1 1/2 cups of heavy whipping cream
- 3/4 cup of granulated sugar
- 1 cup of whole milk

Instructions

1. Mix the heavy cream, milk, sugar, zest, and salt in a medium-sized pot set on top of the stove. Warm over medium-high heat for about 9 minutes or until you see bubbles on top. Whisk every so often. As soon as you see it boil, take it off the heat.
2. In a big bowl, whisk the yolks together. Put the warm cream mixture into the yolks slowly and steadily while whisking to keep the yolks from cooking.
3. Mix it up again and heat it on the stove for three to five minutes until it coats the back of a spoon. In other words, you can drag your finger through the liquid, which will return to the space you made with your finger.
4. Put the lemon juice and mix it in. Using a high-speed blender will give you the best texture and taste. It can be cooled in the fridge or quickly in an ice bath.
5. Place the chilled lemon mix in the one-1/2-quart freezer bowl of an electric ice cream maker. Then, do what the maker says to do.
6. Place the ice cream in a container that can freeze. Put a lid that won't let air in on the ice cream. You can also use plastic wrap or parchment paper. You can freeze it all night or for at least four hours.

1 cup = 250ml
½ " = 125 ml
¼ " = 62.5ml

1 cup = 120g
½ " = 60g
¼ " 30g